P9-BUI-894

Slide 4

Slide 5

Slide 6

STEP 2 Demonstrate the selected brush stroke in a one-sentence painting.

Project the image of the climber. (Slide 4) Explain that a good way to paint an important image is to begin with a simple sentence.

Then show Slide 5, which includes the following sentence:

The mountain climber edged along the cliff.

Model the mental process that writers often use. Tell them you are going to search for interesting details to characterize your climber by using the zoom lens of your mind's eye to move in close on specific parts of the image: the climber's hands, feet, lips, eyes, etc.

Point out that there are hundreds of possible noun/-*ing* absolutes to describe the climber, but you are going to show one that creates a feeling of tension. Project Slide 6, which reads:

Lips quivering, hands shaking, the mountain climber edged along the cliff.

3

Slide 7

TIP How can a teacher collect hundreds of images to work with? First, you can assign each student to bring two images to class from magazines. Specify that they be no smaller than 5 by 6 inches, which is approximately a half page. To help students who don't have magazines at home, get library discards from the school librarian at the beginning of the year and allow students to go through those during lunch, study hall, after school, or even in class. If you have 140 students and they each locate two images, you have 280 images that you can select from to have laminated for a permanent collection. This will provide you with a resource for additional image grammar assignments. You can also photograph these collected images with a digital camera or slide film and project them for class use.

STEP 3 Have students use the brush stroke by painting an image of their own.

Project the image of the surfer. (Slide 7)

Have students complete Absolute Brush Stroke Descriptions 1–4 on page 5 of the Activity Book.

To encourage class participation, offer 5 bonus points to the students who create the best three or four brush strokes with each image. Repeat the bonus option with each of the five different brush strokes, but to avoid giving points to your best students on every image, try one of these strategies:

(1) Once your best writers have accumulated some points, award points to students who create "reasonably good" examples—examples that are a respectable quality, but not necessarily the very best. Be sure not to diminish these awards by telling the class that they are second choices. Rarely will they notice what you've done.

(2) Give the class three images to write about and award points to the best three brush strokes of each image. You can get these additional images from the collection you create, as described in the tip to the left.

(3) Announce to the class that bonus points for the next image they write about will only be awarded to those who have not yet earned any. Be generous with bonus points. The idea is to nurture positive feelings about grammar as well as to teach students how to paint images with grammatical structures.

Once you acquire a collection of images, sort them into categories—action images, character images, setting images, humorous images, etc. Later, you can have students choose a category to use as they practice their brush strokes. This will allow you to give out awards by category and increase the number of students getting positive feedback.

image grammar
ACTIVITY BOOK

 =

HARRY R. NODEN

TEACHER GUIDE

Perfection Learning®

Editorial Director   Julie A. Schumacher
Designer   Emily J. Greazel, Robin Elwick
Image Acquisition   Anjanette Miner

Image Credits

fcv/tp: Iconica / Robert Manella / Getty Images; iii: © Corbis Royalty-Free; iv: iStock; 1: (top) Johner Images / Johner / Getty Images; 1: (bottom) Photos.com; 3: Photonica / Matt Gray; 4: Photonica / John Russell; 6: Photonica; 7–8: Photonica / Jakob Helbig; 10: Photonica / GK& Vikki Hart / Getty Images; 13: (top) Photos.com; 13: (bottom) amana images / Akira Uchiyama / Getty Images; 14: (left) Photonica / Matthias Tunger / Getty Images; 14: (right) © Michael Yelman / SuperStock; 22: Bill Hatcher; 23: N.C. Wyeth (1882–1945) Treasure Island, 1911 Oil on canvas Endpaper illustration for Robert Louis Stevenson, Treasure Island, New York: Charles Scribner's Sons, 1911, Collection of the Brandywine River Museum, Purchased in memory of Hope Montgomery Scott, 1997; 24: Photos.com; 37: Harry Noden © 2005; 40: Photos.com; 41: original drawing © Harry Noden; 45: (top) Photographer's Choice / Brad Rickerby / Getty Images; 45: (bottom) Reportage / Brian Bahr / Getty Images; 49: Harry Noden © 2005; 53: (bottom) iStock.com; 53: (top) Photos.com; 55: Harry Noden © 2005; 83: Photonica / VEER Third Eye Images / Getty Images; bcv: Photos.com

© Copyright 2007 by Perfection Learning® Corporation
1000 North Second Avenue
P.O. Box 500
Logan, Iowa 51546-0500
Tel: 1-800-831-4190 · Fax: 1-800-543-2745
perfectionlearning.com

Printed in the United States of America

 3 4 5 6 7 PP 12 11 10 09 08

75871 ISBN-13: 978-0-7891-7083-5   ISBN-10: 0-7891-7083-3

CONTENTS

CONTENTS continued

Image Grammar Teacher Guide
Painting Brush Strokes

In this Teacher Guide you will find additional explanations, examples, and images to share with students. To make your instruction easier, a PowerPoint presentation is included that works in harmony with the student Activity Book. Throughout this Guide, you will find additional commentary and additional visual clarification for this presentation.

Note that at the end of the PowerPoint CD, you will find a section entitled Advanced Brush Stroke Techniques. This instruction is for your more advanced students.

Slide 1

Slide 2

Slide 3

Teaching students to use brush strokes works best if you follow three critical steps.

STEP 1 Show one or more examples of the selected brush stroke and give students an "extremely oversimplified" definition.

Children acquire much of their grammatical knowledge through imitation. That's why babies can acquire language by simply hearing their mothers read and talk to them. Similarly, by showing your students simple examples of brush strokes and characterizing the brush strokes with "extremely oversimplified definitions," you tap into an important and seldom used teaching tool—imitation.

Begin by having students turn to the graphic organizer on page 2 in their Activity Book. Using the PowerPoint Presentation entitled Painting Brush Strokes, project Slide 1 and then the graphic organizer on Slide 2.

Explain to students that this reference tool—(A Graphic Organizer for the Five Basic Brush Strokes)—is also in their Activity Book and will serve as a guide for creating written brush strokes.

Next, project Slide 3 and review the oversimplified definition of an absolute, pointing out to students that the absolute phrase on the screen can be defined as a noun and an *-ing* word. For example, the word *engine* is a noun and *smoking* is an *-ing* word, creating an absolute. Similarly, the word *gears* is a noun and *grinding* is an *-ing* word, providing a second absolute.

Summarize the explanation of an absolute on page 3 in the student Activity Book, and then tell the class that you are going to demonstrate how to paint one. Emphasize that the writer as an artist uses two different types of perception when painting: (1) the visual eye and (2) the imaginative eye.

The visual eye is what the writer can actually see; the imaginative eye is what the writer imagines. In the description of the car, for example, the artist/writer used "engine smoking" as a detail that he or she might have observed—the visual eye. However, let's assume that the writer was not close enough to hear "gears grinding." He or she may have used the imaginative eye to create that additional detail. Good writers always mix the visual and the imaginative as they write.

Re-emphasize with students that brush stroke commas often function like a zoom lens, encouraging the writer to add close-up details to the image. For example, notice how the writer of the following sentence zooms in on the face of an alligator to paint close-up images.

> **Jaws snapping, teeth grinding, the alligator lunged at the dog.**

For each of the remaining four brush strokes, which we will be examining in the pages ahead, follow the same three-step procedure:

STEP 1 Show one or more examples of the selected brush stroke and give students an "extremely oversimplified" definition.

STEP 2 Demonstrate the selected brush stroke in a one-sentence painting.

STEP 3 Have students use the brush stroke by painting an image of their own.

In the student Activity Book, you will see occasional statements such as, "After your teacher has given you some additional explanation…" These statements refer to the commentary in this Teacher Guide. You may choose to use this commentary or inject commentary of your own.

Slide 8

Teaching students to use brush strokes works best if you follow two critical steps.

STEP 1 Review the example of an appositive in PowerPoint Slide 8.

Then show students an image of a volcano (Slide 9) and demonstrate how one might create a basic sentence about it. (Slide 10)

STEP 2 Point out how a writer might brainstorm for other nouns that could substitute for the word *volcano*.

Slide 9

Give some examples such as *explosion, eruption*, and *detonation*, or characterize the volcano by calling it "a god, a beast, a creature, a weapon, or a machine." Then demonstrate how to embellish an appositive to take full advantage of the brush stroke's double exposure.

For example, you might show how the word *beast* can be expanded to an appositive phrase like "a vicious beast with claws of molten lava." (Slide 11) Point out that any number of images could be created such as "a mindless beast with flaming tentacles."

Slide 10

Have students create a similar sentence, using an appositive, to describe the image of the soldier in their Activity Book, page 6. (Slide 11a)

Slide 11

Slide 11a

Slide 12

STEP 1 Review the example of a participle brush stroke on PowerPoint Slide 12.

Next, using the image of the skier, show students how one might create a basic sentence about the image. (Slides 13 and 14)

STEP 2: Demonstrate how to add a participle brush stroke with an *-ing* phrase. (Slide 15)

Slide 13

Slide 14

Slide 15

Slide 16

Slide 16a

Another option with the participle brush stroke is to use three one-word participles at the beginning or end of a sentence. Show students the model on Slide 16. Remind your class not to paint this brush stroke in the middle of the sentence because it might become absorbed into the verb.

TIP Caution students about the dangling participle. For example, have students visualize the images in this sentence: "Singing, splashing, and laughing, the swimmer attracted the shark." Then show them what happens when the order of words is shifted, creating dangling participles: "Singing, splashing, and laughing, the shark was attracted to the swimmer." Opening participles always link to the noun that follows the zoom lens comma.

STEP 3 Assign the students to write a one-sentence description of the python found on page 8 of the Activity Book and complete the other participle brush stroke descriptions on page 9. (Slide 16a)

Give them the option of using three one-word participle brush strokes or one long participial phrase.

Slide 17

Slide 18

Slide 19

STEP 1 Show students Slide 17 and explain that adjectives out-of-order should be one of the easiest brush strokes to use.

With your class, brainstorm a list of adjectives that might describe a given noun. For example, give them the template on Slide 18.

> The _____, _____, _____ pit bull
> turned toward the intruders.

Then brainstorm for as many adjectives as students can think of and list these on the board or on an overhead.

Finally, have students select three adjectives that they believe best characterize the pit bull, and place those three in the template on Slide 19.

> The _____ pit bull, _____ and _____,
> turned toward the intruders.

Point out how much more powerful the shifted adjectives are, compared to placing them before the noun.

Slide 20

Slide 21

Slide 22

STEP 2 Demonstrate the selected brush stroke in a one-sentence painting.

Show students how adjectives out-of-order can paint an image. Have them brainstorm a list of adjectives to describe the leopard cub pictured in their Activity Book on page 10. (Slides 20 and 21)

After students have written their examples for Description 1 on page 11 of the Activity Book, show them one other possibility. (Slide 22)

STEP 3 Have students use this brush stroke by painting images of their own for Descriptions 2 and 3 on page 11 in the student Activity Book.

Slide 23

Slide 24

Slide 25

Slide 26

Show the students Jon Franklin's quote, which is on Slide 23 and also on page 12 in their Activity Book.

Before students read the explanation on page 12 that tells how action verbs transform still images into action images, try this. Show Slide 24 and then review the concept by asking students to close their eyes and visualize the sentence as you read it.

Do the same with Slide 25.

Point out how the action verb transforms the still picture in their minds into a motion picture.

To further illustrate the power of action verbs, show the version of *Treasure Island* with all of its action verbs removed and *being* verbs inserted in their place. (Slide 26)

Have them rewrite this passage on page 13 of the Activity Book, eliminating as many of the *being* verbs as possible. Caution them not to use any of the following:

Linking and Helping Verbs *is, am, are, was, were, be, being, been, has, have, had, do, does, did, shall, will, should, would, may, might, must, can, could.*

Explain that while helping and *being* verbs are needed at times, fifty to eighty percent of them can usually be removed from a student's rough draft.

Slide 27

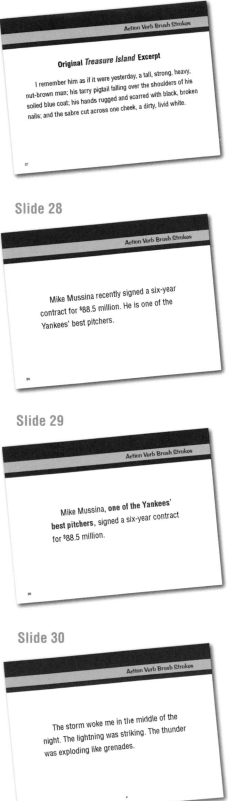

After students rewrite the description from *Treasure Island*, eliminating as many *being* verbs as they can, ask them to share their rewrites. Almost any elimination of *being* verbs will strengthen the passage. However, point out that usually they will not be able to eliminate all of these verbs. In a case where it seems impossible, the verb is probably needed for some purpose such as a definition or clarification.

Then, share with them the original passage as Robert Louis Stevenson wrote it. (Slide 27)

Note how Stevenson used brush strokes as a way of eliminating *being* verbs. Explain to your students that often two sentences can be combined when one contains a linking verb. To illustrate this show the two sentences on Slide 28.

Then show the students on Slide 29 how they can combine these into a single, more powerful sentence, using an absolute structure in place of the *being* verb.

Point out that brush strokes often replace linking verb sentences. For example, a novice might write, "The storm woke me in the middle of the night. The lightning was striking. The thunder was exploding like grenades." (Slide 30)

However, a skilled writer might replace the linking verbs by painting brush strokes. "Lightning striking, thunder exploding like grenades, the storm woke me in the middle of the night." (Slide 31)

Slide 30

Slide 31

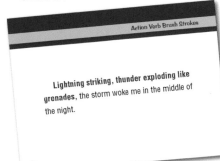

Slide 32

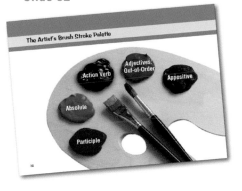

Slide 33

Slide 34

Suggest to your students that if they are uncertain about how any of the brush strokes are created, they should review the two companion graphic organizers. The first is The Artist's Brush Stroke Palette, on page 14 of the Activity Book. **(Slide 32)** It puts the names of the brush strokes on pools of paint on an artist's palette. The other is The Five Basic Brush Strokes graphic on page 2 of the Activity Book, which provides examples of each item on the palette.

Show students **Slide 33**, which is a passage from Ray Bradbury's short story "The Sound of Thunder."

Point out how each color represents a different brush stroke. Blue represents appositives, purple indicates action verbs, red identifies participles, and orange labels absolutes. (This passage has no adjectives out-of-order, although Bradbury often used them.)

Using **Slides 34**, **35**, and **36**, walk students through the process of painting a paragraph about the lioness by adding an appositive (blue) to the first sentence, adding a participle (red) to the second sentence, and adding an absolute (orange) to the third sentence. Note the active verbs in purple.

Show how the brush stroke labels in slide 35 represent the brush strokes inserted in slide 36. Have students note the added power in the brush stroke passage.

Emphasize that this paragraph was constructed using the Artist's Brush Stroke Palette. (See slide 32.) The mind of a professional writer contains a collection of these and other structures that the writer can dip into when painting passages. The palette we are using represents five of the most common grammatical structures used to start students painting detailed word images.

Slide 35

Slide 36

Slide 37

Rubric for the Brush Stroke Paragraph

Name_____ Period____

Each brush stroke used in your paragraph will be worth 10 points. Be sure to label each technique in the margin and draw an arrow to the example.

Absolute _____   Total Points Earned = _____
Appositive _____   Grade = _____
Adjectives Out-of-Order _____
Participle _____
Action Verbs _____

37

Slide 38

For the first assignment using multiple brush strokes, use the rubric on **Slide 37**, which is also in the student Activity Book on page 18. If you grade students only on these five items, holding off on evaluating other grammatical elements, you will not only enable them to have success, but also condition them to working with rubrics that target skills.

Duplicate copies of the rubric and use it as an assessment tool. Try not to evaluate your students on other items—run-ons, usage, etc. Those items can be the focus of later assignments. For now, try to motivate your class to "play" with the art of writing, concentrating on a few items at a time.

You might want to consider borrowing some colored pencils from the art teacher and having your students either underline brush stroke passages or write them in color.

If you decide to do this, use this color code consistent with examples in the Activity Book and PowerPoint slides:

absolutes (orange) **adjectives out-of-order (green)**
appositives (blue) **action verbs (purple)**
participles (red)

Give this assignment for Activity 6 to students:

Try describing one of the two images **(Slide 38)** on page 16 of your Activity Book using all five brush strokes. Create a four- or five-sentence paragraph and label each brush stroke in the margin. Use all five brush strokes, but do not use more than two strokes in a sentence.

As you write, be sure that most of your verbs are active and that they give movement to the action you are describing. *Being* verbs are sometimes needed for definitions and other functions, but nonprofessional writers use far too many, destroying the power of their images.

Sometimes requiring students to complete all five brush strokes can be overwhelming, so you may want to begin with assigning three brush strokes in the paragraph as illustrated with the description of the lioness. With struggling students, have them imitate the paragraph of the lioness with a photo of another animal and specifically require them to use an appositive, a participle, and an absolute—one in each of the three sentences.

This assignment assumes that you may not have created a collection of images as suggested earlier on page 4 of this book. However, if you did and now have a photo collection to work with, use the following assignment instead of the one in the Activity Book.

From the photo collection, distribute three or four images to each student. (If earlier you collected two images from each of your students in each class, you should have enough photos to give each student three or four.) Have students select a favorite image. Allow them to trade images if nothing appeals to them in the samples they are given.

You can use these images in a variety of ways: (1) Post them around the room so students can select an image to write about. (2) Photograph the images to project on screen to supplement in-class demonstrations of brush strokes.

Slide 39

Vocabulary Images of Sue Grafton's Women

keys jingling between her fingers like castanets

high cheekbones *Barely glancing* smiled fleetingly shaggy mane

complexion fresh and clean

eyes darkly charcoaled red

tear-streaked face babbled **one eye cocked** cashmere sweater

makeup smeared frog lips groping blindly false lashes sleeves pushed up

clutched screamy

Fumbling in her handbag for a Kleenex untidy tangle of auburn hair

tantalizing whiff **FLICKED**

halfway down her neck shrugged like someone chewing ice

Slide 40

Vocabulary Images of Sue Grafton's Men

flinging an arm across the back of the chair

bony face **big,** slouched in his seat

sagging cheeks screamy dark eyes

BREATHING HOARSE AND WHEEZY **BLEARY-EYED STARE** attitude of arrogance

dense brow over drooping eyelids hands

padding in his plaid sport coat mustache, trailing down around his mouth parted in his pockets

shaggy corn-yellow hair sauntering

winked *leisurely pace* laced his hands across his head **Perfunctory smile**

hair combed away from his face fragrance of crushed spices

SNAPPED HIS FINGERS

thick brows ruddy complexion

Slide 41

Sample Use of Grafton's Vocabulary Images

Breathing horse and wheezy, Slick Marvin Muggins walked into the restaurant and slouched into his usual chair at a table near the window. A waitress walked by, and he raised his hand, snapped his finger, and shouted "Hey you! Can I get some service here?" She curled her lips in a sneer and sauntered on into the kitchen. Willie's thick eyebrows drooped over his eyelids, and he began rapping his fingers nervously on the table.

"What is wrong with people these days?" Willie said. "They're so rude."

This warm up activity will help students get a feel for the power of combining brush strokes in passages. Having students work in teams increases the excitement and play with grammatical structures and serves as a review.

This is a good place to talk to your students about plagiarism. Explain to them that imitating an author's structures (absolutes, participles, etc.) with words of your own is not unethical and is actually part of how authors learn their craft. Similarly, collecting vocabulary words and short phrases is also valid. These build your image vocabulary. However, copying sentences and paragraphs word per word is considered both unethical and illegal. The difference is that grammatical structures and vocabulary words (even short phrases) are shared by professional authors; copied sentences and passages are not.

To give students a feel for dipping into a word palette, show the palette samples on **Slides 39** and **40** and then the sample passage on **Slide 41**. Emphasize how the samples work to add powerful details to the description.

Point out to students that while Sue Grafton described most of her characters to create suspense, they can adapt these images to write a comic scene, a sad scene, or any other type of emotional encounter. As they develop their scene for Activity 8, they may wish to add a few lines of dialogue as the characters interact. You might suggest they balance the dialogue and description with four or five dialogue lines to every descriptive paragraph.

Slide 42

Brush Stroke Images
**from the Mind
of Jack London**

Both Activities 8 and 9 can be used to help students begin a collection of sketchbook palette samples, described in Activities 10 and 11. Although the collected images in the work of Jack London are organized by brush strokes **(Slides 42–48)**, this can be difficult for some classes.

Slide 43

Brush Strokes from the Mind of Jack London
Absolutes and Absolute Phrases

HAIR BRISTLING   **body flashing forward**   blood flowing from nose and mouth and ears

lips writhing and snarling   *chest panting futilely*

JAWS CLIPPING TOGETHER

Muscles writhing and knotting like live things under his silky fur   ears laid back   eyes diabolically gleaming   **mouth foaming**

Slide 44

Brush Strokes from the Mind of Jack London
Appositives and Noun Phrases

a lawgiver, a master to be obeyed   **slavered fangs**   **blood-shot eyes**

PERPETUAL SNARL   **malignant eye**   ice that bent and crackled under foot

An oath from Perrault—the resounding impact of a club upon a body frame   *warm wet tongue*

Elmo, a huge St. Bernard

Slide 45

Brush Strokes from the Mind of Jack London
Action Verbs and Verb Phrases

sprang for his throat   growled menacingly   sniffed

whirled over   shrieked

choked him   circled   *flung*

taunted him

BRISTLED HIS NECK-HAIR AND SNARLED   wagged his tail

throbbed   crawled to his feet

Slide 46

Brush Strokes from the Mind of Jack London

Participles and Participial Phrases

yelping   pulling till his   **snarling and growing**

sobbing for breath   tendons cracked   BRISTLING

screaming with agony beneath the bristling mass of bodies   gasping painfully for air   surging and wrestling with it

snapping like a demon   **sinking his teeth into it**   shivering

Slide 47

Brush Strokes from the Mind of Jack London

Adjectives Out-of-Order and Adjectives

ruthless   sour and introspective   *mushy*

limp and draggled   **evil-looking**

furry   bloody

ragged and unkempt   lean and gaunt with a battle-scarred face

parched and swollen   swarthy   **mangled**

fierce   *calm and impartial*

Slide 48

Brush Strokes from the Mind of Jack London

Adverbs

ORDERLY   shrewdly

imperiously

obscurely   *mercilessly*

calmly   **furiously**

slyly   *docilely*   *curiously*

aimlessly   instinctively

appeasingly

TIP Invite four or five students with the best examples in each class to copy their passages onto construction paper or poster board. Post these examples around the room.

Depending upon the pace of learning with your particular students, you may want to have them begin by collecting interesting, but unclassified, words from the books, articles, poems, and lyrics they read.

Then you might create your own classifications for additional collections: interesting character images, powerful action images, eye-catching setting images, etc. Encourage students to collect short images: words, phrases, and occasional one-sentence entries, but not long passages. Have students keep their palette samples in their sketchbook (Activity 10) and allow them to dip into their collection and use fifteen to twenty-five percent of their palette sample words when they write.

At some point, divide the class into groups and have them search in a novel they are reading for a different type of brush stroke for comparison and discussion. Finally, you can either assign the entire class the task of collecting brush stroke examples or you can make it a bonus point project.

TIP Assign students to imitate phrases taken from Sue Grafton and Jack London in their sketchbook. For example, they might imitate London's "Hair bristling, mouth foaming" with "eyes gleaming, teeth snapping." Playing with brush strokes and simple image imitations will help nurture their writer's eye for details.

The sketchbook can be combined with a journal or portfolio. Keep in mind that the sketchbook differs from these other forms in that it is built around images and often includes sample sentences and passages from published works to be used as models for discussion.

Whatever design you select, try to engage students in writing assignments that move them from writing about still images (magazine photos, slides, digital images on Web sites, etc.) to writing about actual events (in-class role playing with costumes, sporting events, musical performances, observations at the local mall, nearby zoo, etc.). The underlying purpose of the sketchbook is to help students think of writing as a connecting point to images of life's experiences, real and imagined.

The sketchbook is organized around two categories of word images—original images that students create and found images that they copy from books and magazines. With the original images, you might want to use the brush stroke rubric and require students to practice these techniques. However, with found images, consider two different types of assignments: the first in which students collect any passages that excite them and the second in which students collect only passages that contain at least one technique you have examined. With the second collection, you can, at times, require students to label techniques in the margin. However, it is also important to allow students to explore and even imitate images they cannot yet define.

For this assignment it would be helpful if your students could purchase or construct a folder with two pockets—one for original images and one for found images.

First Entry

This activity is designed to start students collecting and creating written images in their sketchbook. The Record of Original Descriptions, the Record of Found Paragraph Images, and the Record of Found Phrase and Sentence Images are organizing tools. The sketchbook structure will be used in other sections of the Activity Book as students collect examples of parallel structures, specific nouns and verbs, and other writing techniques. However, any composition that you assign can be recorded as part of the sketchbook collection.

Found Image Options

Found images of palette samples can be used in a variety of ways:

(A) A Personal Image Palette Collection

Have students create their own Personal Image Palette, a collection of sample brush strokes found in their reading. You might begin by having them collect images in interesting categories: action images, character images, and setting images as they read assigned and unassigned works. Once their collection has grown, focus their efforts by having them collect sample brush strokes and add them to the Jack London collection that is already categorized.

(B) A Sketchbook Image Swap

Organize an Image Swap where students trade copies of their words and phrases. Have them add the word images they acquire to their personal palette collection.

(C) An Image Vocabulary Lesson

As they read, require students to locate items for their image collections that contain words other students might not know. Have students read sentences in which these words occur, explain the context of the words, and invite other students to add them to their personal palette collections.

(D) A Day of Favorite Images

You might want to consider A Day of Favorite Images in which students bring in a favorite short piece (one half to two pages) of writing to share. This can be anything from a song lyric to a novel excerpt to a letter to the editor. Assign students to bring a copy of their found item for fifteen points, but give each student who volunteers to share an additional ten bonus points for reading their piece aloud. For students who do not want to read but would like to share, offer five bonus points to any volunteer reader and give fifteen points to the student who was reluctant to read his or her passage.

ACTIVITY 11 Record of Found Phrase and Sentence Images, pages 30-31

To help students build their image vocabulary, have them organize their found images and expand their collection into a personal image palette. Treat the collection as though students are artists collecting hues of color to dab and use in their artwork. Depending on their grasp of brush strokes, you can start them collecting by categories: action images, character images, and setting images. If your students have a firm grasp of brush strokes, you can have them organize their found images by brush stroke categories, using the Jack London collection on pages 24–25 as a starter. This works as a vocabulary builder as well as an aid to teaching grammatical structures.

ACTIVITY 12 Use Your Found Images, page 33

Select the percentage of words that you allow students to use in their exercise based on your perception of their vocabulary. The Activity Book suggests twenty percent as a reasonable starting point. However, with struggling students, you might want to begin by allowing students to freely borrow from their palettes and then later limit the percentage. Typically, the images from a student's palette act as a catalyst to generate a larger number of original images.

Advanced Brush Strokes

Advanced brush strokes are difficult for most students. So only a few simple examples are included in the Activity Book to introduce students to higher levels. If you are working with AP or gifted students and wish to introduce a more comprehensive collection of advanced concepts, you will find additional examples at the end of the PowerPoint presentation.

ACTIVITY 13 Paint with a Series of Participles, page 35

Slide 49

Advanced Brush Strokes

The headlight on the bike bounced up and down, jerking the shadows on the terrain ahead, making it difficult to see what was coming.

– Michael Crichton, *Prey*

Introduce the participle series, explaining that it is simply two participle brush strokes in a row. Show **Slide 49**.

Have students imitate Michael Crichton using the photo and core sentence in **Slide 50**. (This photo is also in the student Activity Book on page 34.)

Slide 50

Advanced Brush Strokes

The spotlight on her miner's helmet illuminated the cave, …

ACTIVITY 14 Paint a Participle/Absolute Combination, page 37

Slide 51

Advanced Brush Strokes

A little bit ahead he saw the high-domed shell of a land turtle, crawling slowly along through the dust, its legs working stiffly and jerkily.

— John Steinbeck, *The Grapes of Wrath*

Introduce the participle/absolute combination by showing **Slide 51**.

Have students imitate John Steinbeck's sentence by using the painting by N.C. Wyeth along with the core sentence. **(Slide 52)**

Slide 52

Advanced Brush Strokes

At the head of the charging band of pirates, I spotted Captain Kidd, …

ACTIVITY 15 Experiment with Selected Techniques, page 38

Slide 53

The last exercise in this section of the Activity Book allows students to use simple brush strokes and one or two advanced techniques in a paragraph as they write about the image on page 38 of their book **(Slide 53)**. If your class is gifted, you may want to continue the basic imitation procedure used in the last two activities. Show students a model of an advanced brush stroke, and then have them imitate the structure. You will find a catalog of advanced brush strokes in the Advanced Brush Stroke Techniques at the end of the PowerPoint presentation.

Images to use with these structures can be found at http://www3.uakron.edu/noden. This is the Image Grammar Web site— a companion to the book *Image Grammar*. Here you will not only find images for writing, but also lesson ideas.

Image Grammar Teacher Guide

The Musical Rhythms of Language

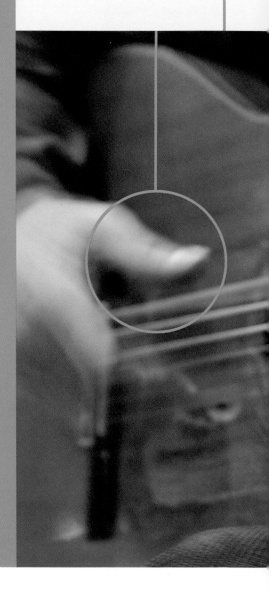

Section 2: The Musical Rhythms of Language

Slide 1

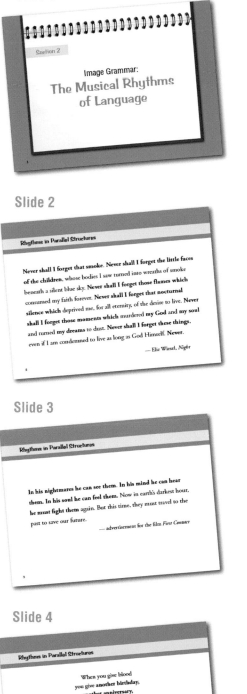

Introduce Section 2 of Image Grammar with **Slide 1** from the PowerPoint presentation.

Introduce the samples of musical rhythms on **Slides 2, 3,** and **4** and read them with an emphasis on the boldfaced words.

Slide 2

Rhythms in Parallel Structures

Never shall I forget that smoke. Never shall I forget the little faces of the children, whose bodies I saw turned into wreaths of smoke beneath a silent blue sky. **Never shall I forget those flames which** consumed my faith forever. **Never shall I forget that nocturnal silence which** deprived me, for all eternity, of the desire to live. **Never shall I forget those moments which** murdered **my God and my soul** and turned **my dreams** to dust. **Never shall I forget these things,** even if I am condemned to live as long as God Himself. **Never.**

— Elie Wiesel, *Night*

Slide 3

Rhythms in Parallel Structures

In his nightmares he can see them. In his mind he can hear them. In his soul he can feel them. Now in earth's darkest hour, **he must fight them** again. But this time, they must travel to the past to save our future.

— advertisement for the film *First Contact*

Slide 4

Rhythms in Parallel Structures

When you give blood
you give **another birthday,**
another anniversary,
another day at the beach,
another night under the stars,
another talk with a friend,
another laugh,
another hug,
another chance.

Please give blood.

— advertisement for the American Red Cross

Feel the Rhythm, page 42

Slide 5

Rhythms in Parallel Structures

Should human cloning be banned?
Should animals have rights?
Should music lyrics be censored?
Should all Americans be required to carry an identity card?
Should high school athletes be required to take drug tests?
Should abortion be outlawed?
Should formal prayer in schools be encouraged?
Should United States immigrants be required to speak English?
Should students be required to wear school uniforms?
Should proficiency tests be abandoned?

Slide 6

Rhythms in Parallel Structures

Should boxing be banned?
Should we abolish the death penalty?
Should the Ten Commandments be displayed in schools?
Should the United States have invaded Iraq?
Should all schools be private and run for profit?
Should we work to halt global warming?
Should we establish free health care for all Americans?
Should laws be passed to limit gun ownership?
Should immoral films, video games, and books be banned?

Slide 7

Rhythms in Parallel Structures

Between what can be seen and what can be feared, between what lives and what never dies, between the light of truth and the darkness of evil lies the future of terror.
— television advertisement for *Lord of Illusions*

Slide 8

Rhythms in Parallel Structures

Between what _____ _____ _____ and
what _____ _____ _____, between
what _____ and what _____,
between the _____ of _____ and the _____
of _____, lies the _____ of _____.

A good way to help students hear and feel the musical rhythms of grammar is to begin with a template exercise. Divide your class into four or five groups and explain that you want them to experience the music of language commonly found in essays.

Have each group select a topic and take a position on it. Explain that with any debatable topic, opinions will differ. So individuals need to compromise and work with the majority perspective. Emphasize that the purpose of this exercise is to experiment with rhythm. The focus is on technique, not topic. Show the topic possibilities on **Slides 5** and **6**, and have each group select one to write about.

After students have selected a topic, show them the advertisement on **Slide 7**, which is also in their Activity Book on page 41. This will be the model for them to imitate.

Next, project the template on **Slide 8** and have students fill in the blanks with words that express their views. Students should feel free to change the number of blanks in the template to match their ideas as long as they keep a rhythm.

Slide 9

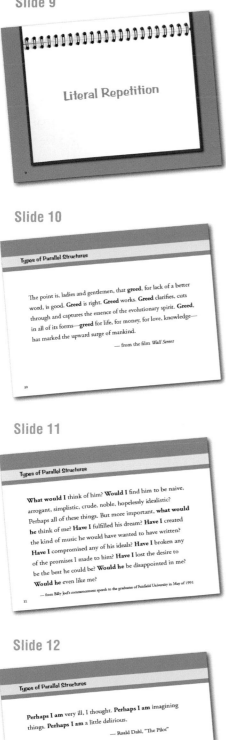

Slide 10

Slide 11

Slide 12

Once the groups have completed the template in Activity 1, have each group select a spokesperson to read its example out loud. After the groups have shared, introduce the various forms of parallel structure: literal, grammatical, and literal and grammatical.

Literal Repetition (Slide 9)

Literal repetitions can be constructed with almost any grammatical structure including nouns, verbs, absolutes, appositives, participles, etc. Any structure can be repeated as the examples on **Slides 10** and **11** illustrate.

Slide 12 shows two more examples that are not in the student Activity Book.

If you wish to reinforce the use of literal repetition, have students analyze Poe's "The Tell-Tale Heart," available online at http://bau2.uibk.ac.at/sg/poe/works/tt_heart.html. As with other links, if this site has changed, just insert the words "The Tell-Tale Heart" in Google.

Slide 13

Pure Grammatical Repetition

Slide 14

Pure Grammatical Repetition

Over the river and **through the woods**, to **grandmother's house**, we go.

Slide 15

Pure Grammatical Repetition

de DAH de DAH de DAH de DAH de DAH,
de DAH de DAH de DAH de DAH de DUM;
de DAH de DAH, de DAH de DAH, de DAH
de DAH, de DAH de DAH de DAH, de DUM.

Slide 16

Pure Grammatical Repetition

Quatrain from Shakespeare's Sonnet 73

That time of year thou mayst in me behold

When yellow leaves, or none, or few, do hang

Upon those boughs which shake against the cold,

Bare ruin'd choirs, where late the sweet birds sang.

Pure Grammatical Repetition

Introduce this type of repetition with **Slide 13**.

Explain that pure grammatical repetition is like the calculus of parallel structure because we have no visual repetitions to help identify it. Using **Slides 14** through **16**, review the examples given in the student Activity Book.

Shakespeare used pure grammatical repetition frequently in both his poems and plays. Share the sound of his most popular rhythm—iambic ("de Dah") pentameter (five beats)—by having student repeat the example on **Slide 15**. Be sure students emphasize the downbeat on the second syllable.

Now have the class read in unison the Shakespeare passage on **Slide 16**, which illustrates the "de Dah" rhythm.

At this point you might mention that about two-thirds of medieval and Renaissance poetry was written in iambic pentameter rhythms. In that period, writers were enthralled with this rhythm and used it not only in poetry, but in plays and songs as well.

If you want to add a formal definition of iambic pentameter, you can define it as an "iambic" rhythm of an unstressed followed by a stressed syllable, repeated five (pentameter) times.

Slide 17

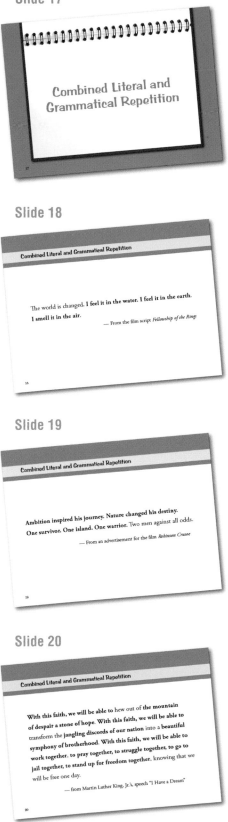

Slide 17 — Combined Literal and Grammatical Repetition

Slide 18

Combined Literal and Grammatical Repetition

The world is changed. I feel it in the water. I feel it in the earth. I smell it in the air.
— From the film script *Fellowship of the Rings*

Slide 19

Combined Literal and Grammatical Repetition

Ambition inspired his journey. Nature changed his destiny. One survivor. One island. One warrior. Two men against all odds.
— From an advertisement for the film *Robinson Crusoe*

Slide 20

Combined Literal and Grammatical Repetition

With this faith, we will be able to hew out of the mountain of despair a stone of hope. With this faith, we will be able to transform the jangling discords of our nation into a beautiful symphony of brotherhood. With this faith, we will be able to work together, to pray together, to struggle together, to go to jail together, to stand up for freedom together, knowing that we will be free one day.
— from Martin Luther King, Jr.'s speech "I Have a Dream"

Combined Literal and Grammatical Repetition

Introduce this pattern with **Slide 17**.

Combining literal and grammatical patterns is one of the most effective and frequently used rhythm techniques.

Notice that part of the repetition in the script from *The Fellowship of the Rings* (**Slide 18**) relies on literal repetition: "I feel it in the…," and part of the passage repeats a grammatical structure (a prepositional phrase), but changes the final word with each phrase: "in the water, in the earth, in the air."

On **Slide 19**, the first two sentences repeat the following grammatical pattern: "noun verb [his] noun." The second three phrases repeat the word "One," and then alter the noun that follows. You may want to note that the scriptwriter in these three phrases uses fragments to enhance the emphasis.

Students will no doubt be familiar with the passage from Dr. King's speech (**Slide 20**). Ask them to point out the repetition patterns in this excerpt.

Additional Activity Options

A Rhythm Hunt

Consider having students locate an interesting speech at the American Rhetoric site (http://www.americanrhetoric.com/top100speechesall.html) to help them further realize the power and frequent use of repetition. American Rhetoric is an excellent source of sample speeches, almost all of which are loaded with rhythmic examples. The site contains a variety of speeches "from movies, sermons, popular songs, and sensational media events by famous (and infamous) politicians, actors, religious leaders, athletes, singers, and other noteworthy personalities." Some of the speeches available include John Fitzgerald Kennedy's "Inaugural Address," Franklin Delano Roosevelt's "First Inaugural Address," Malcolm X's "The Ballot or the Bullet," and Ronald Reagan's *Challenger* Address. All contain excellent examples of parallel structure.

Require students to locate three or four specific rhythmic passages from the speech they select. Many of the speeches are recorded in mp3 formats and can be downloaded or played. You may want to have students listen to several speeches as part of their search. Sometimes hearing a speech makes it easier for students to identify rhythms.

(Of course, if you have difficulty locating it, simply insert "American rhetoric, speeches," or "top speeches" into a Google search, and you will find this site or other similar ones.)

Rhythm Hunt Group Activity

You might also want to consider having groups of students examine a single speech in its entirety. If so, divide the class into four or five teams and give each team a different speech to analyze. Next, have each team elect a recorder who will write the names of team members on one copy of the speech and keep track of the examples the group finds.

Explain to the teams that they will have fifteen minutes to locate and identify six rhythms (two of each type: literal, literal/grammatical, and pure grammatical) in their speech. When any member of the group spots an example, he or she should tell the group recorder who will highlight or circle the example on his or her copy.

Additional Activity Options (cont.)

Finally, signal the groups to begin, and time them. If any team finishes before the fifteen minutes has elapsed, the group should review their answers to be sure they have two examples in each category. At the conclusion of the competition, collect the team sheets and award each team ten points for each item located—five points for an example of a parallel structure and five points for the correct identification of the example. Give teams partial credit if they locate a parallel structure but can't identify which type it is.

To create a competitive feeling of suspense, score one item at a time for each team, announcing the example and the identification. Keep a running score as you evaluate the first answer for each team in turn. Award the winning team bonus points and post their team score sheet on the bulletin board so they get recognition for their efforts. (If you find it difficult to analyze and announce answers immediately after students turn in their results, you can hold the paper submitted by each group until the next day. This would give you more time to check answers and devise some type of dramatic announcement.)

An Argumentative Theme

You might also want to consider having your students use their group statement (Activity 1: Feel the Rhythm) as an introduction to a short theme supporting or opposing a topic of their choice. For additional arguments pro and con on these and other topics, encourage students to go online to http://www.debatabase.org/alphaindex.asp. If your students do not have access to a computer lab at school, consider having them collect supporting details for their paragraphs from school and local libraries.

Slide 21

Rod Serling's *Twilight Zone*

The Sports Zone   The Nature Zone   The Music Zone   The Human Trait Zone
The Political Zone   The Crime Zone   The School Zone   The Job Zone

Or you may want to use more specific categories such as

The Steelers Zone   The Eagle Zone   The Broncos Zone   The Gator Zone
The Skateboard Zone   The Forex Zone   The Martial Arts Zone   The Everest Zone
The Rap Zone   The Desert Zone   The Bluegrass Zone   The Love Zone
The Rock Zone   The Hate Zone   The Math Zone   The Friendship Zone
The English Zone   The Car Wash Zone   The Cafeteria Zone   The Burger Cook Zone
The Republican / Democratic Zone

Slide 22

Rod Serling's *Twilight Zone*

There is a fifth dimension beyond that which is known to man.
It is a dimension as vast as space and as timeless as infinity. It is
the middle ground between light and shadow, between science
and superstition, and it lies between the pit of man's fears, and the
summit of his knowledge. This is the dimension of imagination.
It is an area which we call . . . THE TWILIGHT ZONE.

Slide 23

Feel the Rhythms of the *Twilight Zone*

The _____ Zone

There is a fifth dimension beyond that which is known to man. It is a
dimension as _____ as _____ and as _____
as _____. It is the _____ _____ between
as _____ and _____, between _____ and
_____, and it lies between the _____ of _____
_____, and the _____ of his/her _____.
This is the dimension of _____. It is an area which we call . . .
THE _____ ZONE.

Award-winning playwright and author Rod Serling wrote many of the scripts as well as the introduction and conclusion to the old television show the *Twilight Zone*. Using Serling's best known *Twilight Zone* introduction, this exercise gives students an opportunity to feel the rhythms of parallel structure while creating a commentary of their own.

This exercise can be done as a solo or group activity. As instructed in the Activity Book, have students select a topic. Show **Slide 21**, and then complete the template. Next, share with the class the original Serling introduction on **Slide 22**.

Explain to students that their task will be to complete the template (**Slide 23**). Encourage the class to brainstorm multiple ideas for each of the blanks and select the words that create the most interesting ideas.

Whether you do this with groups or with individual students, be sure to allow students an evening to revise and sharpen their templates before inviting them to share examples with the class.

If you want to create a template from a model passage your students are reading, follow these three steps:

1. Select a passage that contains parallel structures.
2. Extract the pattern, leaving nothing but the structural words.
3. Have students imitate the pattern by filling in their own words.

To further help your students understand rhythms, copy and distribute the two-page handout that follows. It contains a wide variety of examples.

These and other examples can be viewed at http://www.americanrhetoric.com/MovieSpeeches/moviespeechnixon3.html.

With the excerpts from Tennyson's poem, invite the students to feel the rhythm by pounding a beat on their desk. The first two-line excerpt creates the feel of galloping horses with a "Boom ta ta, Boom ta ta, Boom ta ta, Boom Boom" rhythm. The last four lines create a "Boom ta ta, Boom ta ta" pattern but end with a "Boom ta ta, Boom ta" line.

Sample Word Rhythms

Musical rhythms occur in every genre: fiction, nonfiction, poetry, advertising, song lyrics, screenplays, and so forth. Here are a few examples to help you feel the rhythms of language.

A Cheerleading Rhythm

Hey, hey, hey, time to fight.
Knock 'em down, blue and white.
Hey, hey, hey, hear us roar.
Go team go, score, score, score.

An Army Cadence

Airborne Rangers with a black beret
kamikaze killers and we earn our pay
jumpin' out of airplanes, runnin' through the swamp,
Uncle Sam's in trouble, Rangers gonna' stomp.
Our minds are like computers, our fists are like steel,
If one doesn't get you, the other one will.

from The Charge of the Light Brigade
by Alfred, Lord Tennyson

Half a league, half a league,
Half a league onward,
              * * *
Cannon to right of them,
Cannon to left of them,
Cannon in front of them
Volley'd and thunder'd;

Sample Word Rhythms

Musical Rhythms from Political Speeches

from George W. Bush's Speech at the 2004 Republican Convention

We see America's character in our military, **which** finds a way or makes one. **We see it in our** veterans, **who are** supporting military families in their days of worry. **We see it in our** young people, **who have** found heroes once again. **We see that character in** workers and entrepreneurs, **who are** renewing our economy with their effort and optimism.

from John Kerry's Speech at the 2004 Democratic National Convention

What does it mean in America today when Dave McCune, a steel worker I met in Canton, Ohio, saw his job sent overseas, and the equipment in his factory literally unbolted, crated up, and shipped thousands of miles away along with that job? **What does it mean** when workers I've met had to train their foreign replacements? **America can do better. And tonight we say: help is on the way.**

What does it mean when Mary Ann Knowles, a woman with breast cancer I met in New Hampshire, had to keep working day after day through her chemotherapy, no matter how sick she felt, because she was terrified of losing her family's health insurance? **America can do better. And help is on the way.**

What does it mean when Deborah Kromins from Philadelphia, Pennsylvania, works and she saves all her life and she finds out that her pension has disappeared into thin air, and the executive who looted it has bailed out on a golden parachute? **America can do better. And help is on the way.**

Musical Rhythms from the Screenplay *Nixon*
(An adaptation of President Richard Nixon's speech to his staff after resigning the presidency)

You see, we think sometimes **when** things happen that don't go the right way, we think that **when** someone dear to us dies, **when** we lose an election, or **when** we suffer defeat, that all is ended. Not true. It's only a beginning, always, because the greatness comes **not when** things go always good for you, **but** the greatness comes **when** you're really tested, **when** you take **some** knocks, **some** disappointments, **when** sadness comes. Because only if you've been in the deepest valley can you ever know how magnificent it is to be on the highest mountain.

Slide 24

Rhythms Using Prepositions

Slide 25

Rhythms Using Prepositions

The cosmos is rich beyond measure—**in** elegant facts, **in** exquisite interrelationships, **in** the subtle machinery of awe.
— Carl Sagan, *Cosmos*

Slide 26

Rhythms Using Prepositions

And so let freedom ring **from** the prodigious hilltops of New Hampshire. Let freedom ring **from** the mighty mountains of New York. Let freedom ring **from** the heightening Alleghenies of Pennsylvania. Let freedom ring **from** the snow-capped Rockies of Colorado. Let freedom ring **from** the curvaceous slopes of California.
— from Martin Luther King, Jr.'s, speech "I Have a Dream"

Slide 27

Rhythms Using Prepositions

1 _____ _____
is rich beyond measure—**in** _____
_____, **in** _____
_____, **in** the _____
_____ **of** _____

Introduce this activity with **Slide 24**.

The idea that musical rhythms come in all kinds of grammatical shapes might overwhelm your students. However, you can show them a few patterns based on simple grammatical structures such as prepositions. Here is a list of the prepositions that are most often used to create melodies. (This list is also in the student book on page 48.)

about, above, across, after, against, along, amid, around, at, before, below, beneath, beside, between, beyond, by, down, for, from, in, into, like, near, of, on, onto, outside, over, through, to, toward, under, underneath, until, with, without

Of course, there are other prepositions in addition to these, but others don't create rhythms as effectively. Share several examples of prepositions creating a beat **(Slides 25** and **26)**.

King also repeats the phrase "let freedom ring" to enhance the rhythm's power even further.

As they begin Activity 3, encourage students to connect to something they enjoy—a hobby, an art form, a sport, a television show, a film, or a musical experience.

Remind the class that there are other prepositions in addition to those listed in their Activity Book, but the listed prepositions can create a more hypnotic effect with combinations such as "of the people, by the people, for the people." Then have students complete the Activity 3 exercise template **(Slide 27)**.

For the second exercise in Activity 3, show **Slide 28**, which is also in the Activity Book, to illustrate how three prepositions can be used to create a rhythm. Assign students to create a similar grammatical pattern with three prepositions of their own in the space provided.

Slide 28

Rhythms Using Prepositions

"**Beyond** Raber's farm, **along** the High Ridge Woods, **near** a grove of red maple trees, lies a little-known trout stream."

ACTIVITY 4 Create a Pattern with a Subordinate Conjunction, page 51

Slide 29

Slide 30

Slide 31

Slide 32

Introduce this activity with **Slide 29**.

With relative pronouns and subordinate conjunctions, rhythms are longer, stretching from long sentences to paragraphs. Patterns of parallel structure provide a good way to introduce students to the power of these two grammatical categories. The Activity Book provides the lists shown on **Slide 30**.

Decades ago, memorizing lists like this was a common teaching tool. However, we now know that students will remember these words longer if they use them in the course of their writing and see them used in the writing of others. Here are a few examples **(Slides 31** to **34)**.

Slide 33

Slide 34

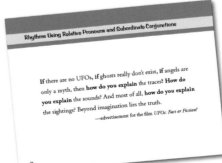

Create a Pattern with a
Subordinate Conjunction, page 51 (cont.)

Slide 35

Slide 36

An image can be a powerful catalyst, inspiring students to seek out details that help shape their ideas. Before students begin Activity 4, encourage them to examine the photograph of the interlocking archways made of stone (Slide 35). Tell them to let their imaginations wander, picturing what type of place this might be or might once have been. You might have the class brainstorm some possibilities orally. Then invite students to either build on an idea from the brainstorm or create another idea of their own, filling in the exercise template (Slide 36).

Note: This is a photograph of the back entrance to the Alamo.

ACTIVITY 5 Create a Pattern with a Relative Pronoun, page 52

Slide 37

Slide 38

Show Slide 37 to your students and ask them to imagine what this street artist might have sacrificed to practice his art. What sort of beliefs might he have? What sort of individual might he be? What specific decisions might he have made to be true to his art? Have your students complete the template (Slide 38) by describing the street artist. Tell students that they should use their imaginative eye to create details about him.

Additional Activity Options

Create a Lyrics Display

Have students collect sample rhythmic lyrics from two or three of their favorite songs. (Tell students to keep in mind that their samples must be appropriate to share in class.)

Bonus Point Option: Invite students who bring the best examples to help design a display of the "Best Parallel Structure Lyrics" on a bulletin board, identifying both the songwriter and the student who located the words. As incentive, offer a few bonus points for anyone interested in working on the display.

Create a Rhythmic Advertisement for a Film

Consider having groups of students compete by creating the best original rhythmic film advertisement for a recent film. Give ten bonus points to the team that creates the best rhythmic ad.

ACTIVITY 6 Create a "Good Old Days" Passage, page 53

If you have access to a computer lab, you can have your entire class gather information for this activity from the Internet. The following page contains some Web sites that should provide enough information for the exercise.

However, if you do not have computer access, consider checking out books from both your public library and your school library to be used in class as a resource. Two recommended historical collections by Time-Life—*Our American Century* and *This Fabulous Century*—are organized with separate volumes dedicated to each decade.

You might also have students research together at group stations. Because most of your students' parents or grandparents were probably born within five or ten years of each other, materials about certain time periods could be at key places in the room for students to share. For example, 60s material could be at one table, the 70s at another, and so forth.

Web Resources for the "Good Old Days" Activity

1950s

In the 50s
http://www.inthe50s.com/contents/complete20.php

Flashback to the 50s
http://www.1950sflashback.com/

Fashions
http://www.costumegallery.com/1950.htm

Literature and Culture of the 1950s
http://www.writing.upenn.edu/~afilreis/50s/home.html

1960s

Timeline
http://www.inthe60s.com/timeline.shtml

Flashback to the 60s
http://www.1960sflashback.com/

Fashions
http://www.costumegallery.com/1960.htm

Cultural History
http://kclibrary.nhmccd.edu/decade60.html

1960s Slang
http://cougartown.com/slang.html

1970s

Timeline
http://www.inthe70s.com/timeline.shtml

Flashback to the 70s
http://www.1970sflashback.com/

Fashions
http://www.costumegallery.com/1970.htm

I Love the 70s
http://www.bbc.co.uk/cult/ilove/years/70sindex.shtml

1980s

Timeline
http://www.inthe80s.com/timeline.shtml

Flashback to the 80s
http://www.1980sflashback.com/

Fashions
http://www.costumegallery.com/1980.htm

Cultural History
http://kclibrary.nhmccd.edu/decade80.html

1990s

Timeline
http://www.inthe90s.com/index.shtml

Flashback to the 90s
http://www.1990sflashback.com/

Fashions
http://www.costumegallery.com/1990.htm

Cultural History
http://kclibrary.nhmccd.edu/decade90.html

Be sure to caution students that Web sites change frequently. If Web sites change, simply enter several key words (cultural history, fifties, seventies, timeline, etc.) into Google and search.

Image Grammar Teacher Guide
Specific Details: The Close-up Power of the Zoom Lens

Section 3: The Close-up Power of the Zoom Lens

Slide 1

Slide 2

Slide 3

Slide 4

Introduce this section of the book with **Slide 1**.

Read the following excerpt to the class.

> **Once upon a point in time, a small person named Little Red Riding Hood initiated plans for the preparation, delivery, and transportation of foodstuffs to her grandmother, a senior citizen residing in a place of residence in a forest of indeterminate dimension.**
>
> **In the process of implementing this program, her incursion into the forest was in mid-transportation process when it attained interface with an alleged perpetrator. This individual, a wolf, made inquiry as to the whereabouts of Little Red Riding Hood's goal as well as inferring that he was desirous of ascertaining the contents of Little Red Riding Hood's foodstuffs basket.**
>
> —Russell Baker, "Little Red Riding Hood"

Ask students why this version of "Little Red Riding Hood" sounds so strange. Someone will probably suggest that the language is complex and hard to understand. Tell them that the author, Russell Baker, was trying to show what happens when we use abstract language—words that fail to paint specific images.

Next, share the quote by John Braine (**Slide 2**), a popular novelist in the 1950s who wrote the best selling novel *Room at the Top*.

Then, illustrate the central concept in Stuart Chase's book *Tyranny of Words* with **Slide 3**, showing the "Levels of Abstraction" as a ladder.

For an amusing activity to illustrate abstract language, share the *Mad Magazine* excerpt on **Slide 4** about taking an essay exam. It illustrates how highly abstract words can sound profound, but mean absolutely nothing.

Slide 5

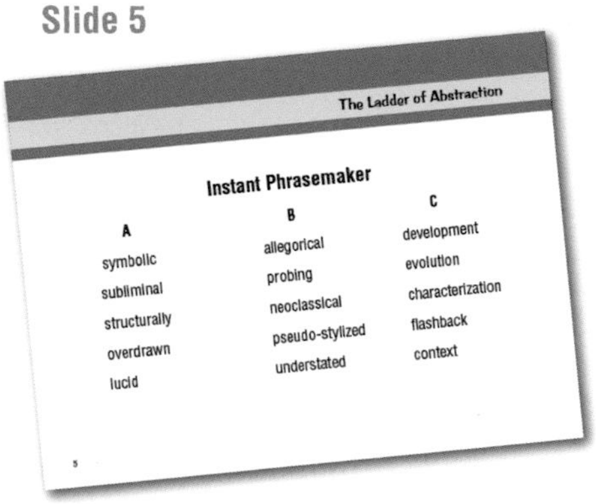

The Ladder of Abstraction

Instant Phrasemaker

A	B	C
symbolic	allegorical	development
subliminal	probing	evolution
structurally	neoclassical	characterization
overdrawn	pseudo-stylized	flashback
lucid	understated	context

Slide 6

The Ladder of Abstraction

No long, involved response to this question is deemed necessary. The author's **structurally allegorical evolution** speaks for itself.

A second or even third reading of this work is recommended to point up its reliance on the classic device of **symbolic neoclassical characterization**.

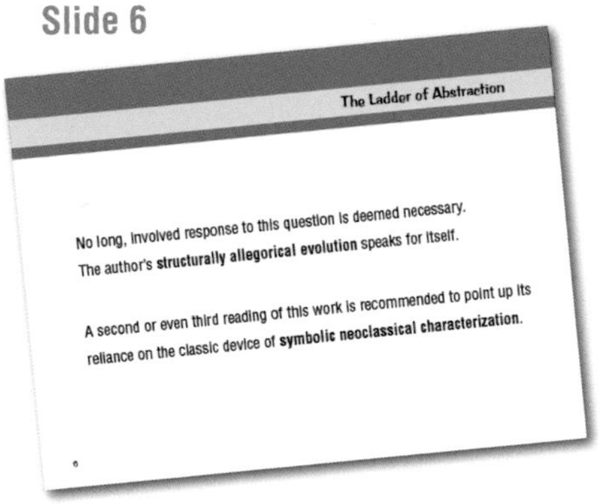

Begin by asking your class to imagine that they are scheduled to take an essay exam about a piece of literature they haven't read and suggest they try using *Mad Magazine's* Instant Phrasemaker **(Slide 5)** by selecting words from columns A, B, and C to fill in the blanks of slide 4.

The result will be statements like those in **Slide 6**. These statements seem impressive, but are hollow—filled with highly abstract words that sound profound but offer no specific images or detailed information. Politicians often find refuge in abstract statements because they hide their true position on issues. A political candidate can say, "I'm in favor of a strong economy." But what does that mean in the daily life of voters? Will that politician support or oppose an increase in taxes on imports? And how will that result in a better economic life for the citizens? Abstractions mask specific meanings.

General semanticists have identified in the structure of our language a hierarchy, which is described in the student Activitiy Book on page 56. They call this hierarchy "levels of abstraction." Having students view this as a ladder simplifies the concept.

Sort the Levels, pages 57-58

Slide 7

> **The Ladder of Abstraction**
>
> **Activity 1: Sort the Levels**
> Unscramble each list on a ladder of abstraction.
>
> **Word List 1**
> creature   dog   St. Bernard   animal   Cujo
>
> **Word List 2**
> public asset   book   *The Sherlock Holmes Reader*   novel   library material
>
> **Word List 3**
> dessert   half-gallon of fudge ripple   ice cream   food   store inventory
>
> **Word List 4**
> *Star Wars IV*   sci-fi film   movie   George Lucas flick   entertainment

Slide 8

> **The Ladder of Abstraction**
>
> **Solutions to Activity 1**
> (highest to lowest)
>
> **Word List 1**
> creature   animal   dog   St. Bernard   Cujo
>
> **Word List 2**
> public asset   library material   book   novel   *The Sherlock Holmes Reader*
>
> **Word List 3**
> store inventory   food   dessert   ice cream   half-gallon of fudge ripple
>
> **Word List 4**
> entertainment   movie   sci-fi film   George Lucas flick   *Star Wars IV*

To help students understand the concept of abstraction, have them unscramble the word lists on pages 57 and 58 of their Activity Book, which are also shown on **Slide 7**. Ask them to arrange the words from most abstract to least abstract. The correct answers for this activity are on **Slide 8**.

As an extension of Activity 1, ask students to scramble the order of their original word list from item 5, and ask a partner to put these words back into correct order.

Point out, that as Braine suggests in Slide 2, a major goal in writing is to use the most specific word, the word on the lowest level of abstraction. Show students the Waddle abstraction in Slide 3 again. Mention that Ezra Pound's two words of advice to Ernest Hemingway about writing were "avoid abstractions."

Painting a Noun Collage with Specific Images, page 59

Slide 9

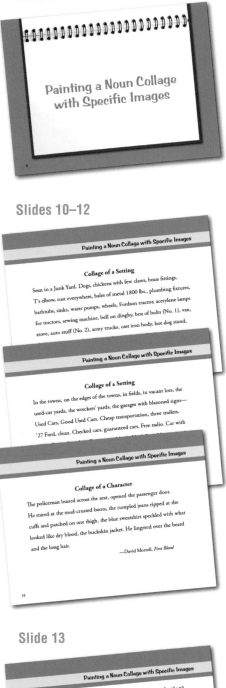

Slides 10–12

Introduce this idea with **Slide 9**. Then, review **Slides 10** to **14** to show students how a "noun collage" can be used to identify a character, a setting, or even a symbolic object. Explain that a noun collage is similar to a collage in art where artists combine a variety of fragmented images to create a unified feeling. Similarly in writing, authors combine a variety of noun images (often sentence fragments) to create a single impression.

Show the class how the collage technique can be used for humor as well by sharing the example on **Slide 14** from Steve Martin's book *Pure Drivel* (Hyperiod Press, New York, 1998, p. 55). Notice how Martin creates humor with the boldfaced specific nouns.

Slide 14

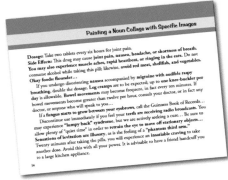

Slide 13

Slide 15

Slide 16

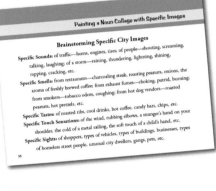

Slide 17

For Activity 2, explain to students that they will not only need to look at the details in each image on page 60 of their books but will also need to use their "imaginative eye" to describe items not seen in the photographs. All authors use this blend of the visual with the imaginative. With the collage paragraph this blend is a necessity.

Demonstrate to students how to brainstorm categories of specific images with the city image on Slide 15, using sensory categories. Explain that the sensory categories (sound, smell, taste, touch, sight) are abstractions that need specific images to bring them alive. (Slide 16)

After demonstrating some examples from the city image, have students brainstorm specific images about the football fans on Slide 17, which is also in their Activity Book. Again use the categories of sound, smell, taste, touch, and sight, and use the same format as you did with the city image.

Brainstorming Specific Football Fan Images

Specific Sounds

Specific Smells

Specific Tastes

Specific Touch Sensations

Specific Sights

Zooming and Layering, pages 62-63

Slide 18

Paint by Zooming and Layering

Introduce this section of the Activity Book with **Slide 18**. Review the explanations of zooming and layering on page 62. Mention that for use with the zoom lens, writers most often use nouns and verbs. Similarly, layering—while it can be done with any type of grammatical structure—works best with brush strokes, adjectives, and prepositional phrases. Demonstrate the difference between zooming and layering with the examples on **Slides 19–26**. To help clarify layering, walk students through each category separately to avoid confusion.

Slide 19

Paint by Zooming and Layering

Rough Draft

The boat went through the waves on the lake. The waves were high and came down. The storm made our minds fearful.

Zooming in on Nouns and Verbs

The rowboat plunged into the waves on Lake Erie. White caps crested and then cascaded. The rain and lightning rippled our minds fearful.

Slide 20

Paint by Zooming and Layering

Types of Layering

Participle Brush Strokes
  swirling above the boat, dancing like the wings of vultures
Absolute Brush Strokes
  hull groaning, oars creaking, water sloshing
Adjectives and/or Adjectives Out-of-Order
  leaky, old, wooden, five-foot, rickety, relentless
Appositives
  old wooden Acme Skiff
Prepositional Phrases
  in the moonlight, into the five-foot waves, upon us

Slide 21

Paint by Zooming and Layering

Layering a Participle Brush Stroke

The rowboat plunged into the waves on Lake Erie. Swirling above the boat, dancing like the wings of vultures, white caps crested and then cascaded. The rain and lightning rippled our minds with fear.

Slide 22

Paint by Zooming and Layering

Layering an Absolute Brush Stroke

Hull groaning, the rowboat plunged into the waves on Lake Erie. Swirling above the boat, dancing like the wings of vultures, white caps crested and then cascaded. The rain and lightning rippled our minds with fear.

Slide 23

Paint by Zooming and Layering

Layering Adjectives and/or Adjectives Out-of-Order

Hull groaning, the leaky rowboat plunged into the five-foot waves on Lake Erie. Swirling above the boat, dancing like the wings of vultures, white caps crested and then cascaded. The relentless rain and lightning rippled our minds with fear.

Slide 24

Paint by Zooming and Layering

Layering with an Appositive Brush Stroke

Hull groaning, the leaky rowboat, an old wooden Acme Skiff, plunged into the five-foot waves on Lake Erie. Swirling above the boat, dancing like the wings of vultures, white caps crested and then cascaded. The relentless rain and lightning rippled our minds with fear.

Slide 25

Paint by Zooming and Layering

Layering with Prepositional Phrases

Hull groaning, the leaky rowboat, an old wooden Acme Skiff, plunged into the five-foot waves on Lake Erie. Swirling above the boat, dancing like the wings of vultures, white caps crested in the moonlight and then cascaded upon us. The relentless rain and lightning rippled our minds with fear.

Slide 26

Paint by Zooming and Layering

Layering after Zooming: Final Draft

Hull groaning, the leaky rowboat, an old wooden Acme Skiff, plunged into the five-foot waves on Lake Erie. Swirling above the boat, dancing like the wings of vultures, white caps crested in the moonlight and then cascaded upon us. The relentless rain and lightning rippled our minds with fear.

Zooming and Layering, pages 62-63 (cont.)

Paint by Zooming and Layering

The pilot, **a man**, volunteered for combat.

The pilot, **an elderly old man with a toothless grin**, volunteered for combat.

Paint by Zooming and Layering

Sniffing, the kitten awoke and trotted toward the kitchen.

Sniffing the aroma of a tuna casserole, the kitten awoke and trotted toward the kitchen.

After reviewing the process of zooming and layering, illustrate how with a first or second draft, participles and appositives can be expanded from single words to phrases. For example, a draft might contain an appositive like the first sentence in Slide 27. Explain that the appositive word *man* can be embellished into an appositive phrase as shown in the second sentence. Similarly, the participle brush stroke can be expanded with more specific images as the two sentences on Slide 28 illustrate.

An excellent resource to illustrate the noun collage is *The Things They Carried* by Tim O'Brien. In this excerpt, O'Brien mixes concrete items with a few abstract nouns to capture the images of soldiers at war.

> **They carried Sterno, safety pins, trip flares,
> signal flares, spools of wire, razor blades …
> They carried infections. They carried the sky.**

Slide 29

> **Paint by Zooming and Layering**
>
> **First Draft**
>
> I always got up in the dark as I do now and my chore, from the time I was eight or so until I went to college at 18, was to see if Grandma was still alive. She'd had a shock—what we'd call a stroke—and had been sent to bed for the rest of her life.

Slide 30

> **Paint by Zooming and Layering**
>
> **Layered Draft**
>
> I always woke in the dark, lay in bed listening to the sounds of family—my mother's heavy turning over, my father's bassoon snore, the clatter of the milkman, the trolley screech grow louder, louder, then quieter, quieter as it passed down Hancock Street. I would get up in the dark by myself as I do now, enjoying the aloneness that is central to my life. My first morning chore, before the paper route, was to see if Grandma lived through the night. She'd had a shock—what we'd now call a stroke—and had been sent to bed for the rest of her life.

Slide 31

> **Paint by Zooming and Layering**
>
> The **creature** **went** into the **water** and **moved** past the **woman**.
>
> With the **dog** close behind him, the **cat** **went** over the fence and **ran** up a **tree** to safety.

To give your students more practice, have them work with the sentences in Activity 3, following the same procedure demonstrated in slides 19 to 26.

You might also want to share the following two items written by Donald Murray in an e-mail to participants in the National Writing Project. Murray explained that he started life as an oil painter, and when he switched his career to writing, borrowed the concept of layering from his experience with oil paints.

Just as artists layer in specific details onto their paintings with paint, Murray layers details with words. He adds words and phrases to give greater detail to his writing. Here is an example of Murray's layering. The first passage (Slide 29) is a rough draft from his book, *Twice-Lived Life*.

The second passage (Slide 30) is his revision with the layered examples highlighted in blue.

You can show the sentences on Slide 31 if you choose to have your students do this activity in class, or you can skip this if you prefer to have your students work on these at home.

Slide 32

Show students **Slide 32** of Bai Yun and Su Lin. Have them write a very short paragraph describing what they see and what they imagine might have occurred immediately after the photo was taken. Next, have them create a long descriptive paragraph using the techniques of zooming and layering.

Creating Humor with Specific Images, pages 68-69

Slide 33

Creating Humor
with Specific Images

Introduce this section with **Slide 33**.

Review the information on page 68 of the student book that explains how specific details can create humor. **Slides 34–37** illustrate how omitting specific images eliminates humor.

Sports announcers use a technique similar to that of humorists called "color commentary." For example, John Madden could have made the general statement on **Slide 38**. But instead he provided the specific image on **Slide 39**.

Slide 40 shows a similar pair of sentences by Jim Murray, the Pulitzer Prize-winning sports columnist.

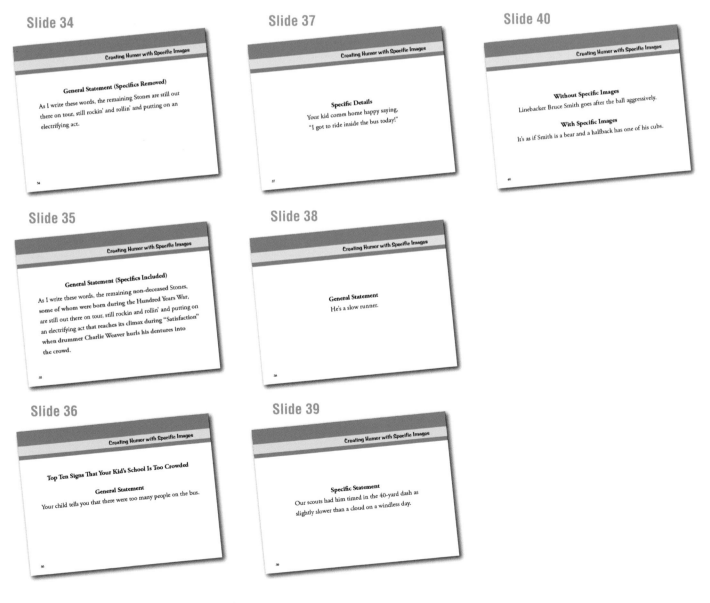

Slide 34

Creating Humor with Specific Images

General Statement (Specifics Removed)

As I write these words, the remaining Stones are still out there on tour, still rockin' and rollin' and putting on an electrifying act.

Slide 37

Creating Humor with Specific Images

Specific Details

Your kid comes home happy saying,
"I got to ride inside the bus today!"

Slide 40

Creating Humor with Specific Images

Without Specific Images

Linebacker Bruce Smith goes after the ball aggressively.

With Specific Images

It's as if Smith is a bear and a halfback has one of his cubs.

Slide 35

Creating Humor with Specific Images

General Statement (Specifics Included)

As I write these words, the remaining non-deceased Stones, some of whom were born during the Hundred Years War, are still out there on tour, still rockin and rollin' and putting on an electrifying act that reaches its climax during "Satisfaction" when drummer Charlie Weaver hurls his dentures into the crowd.

Slide 38

Creating Humor with Specific Images

General Statement

He's a slow runner.

Slide 36

Creating Humor with Specific Images

Top Ten Signs That Your Kid's School Is Too Crowded

General Statement

Your child tells you that there were too many people on the bus.

Slide 39

Creating Humor with Specific Images

Specific Statement

Our scouts had him timed in the 40-yard dash as slightly slower than a cloud on a windless day.

Slide 41

> **Creating Humor with Specific Images**
>
> **General Statement**
> He is hard to tackle.
>
> **Specific Examples with Similes**
> It's like tackling a locomotive.
> —Glen Holtzman
>
> It's like standing blindfolded in the middle of Interstate 75, dodging the cars and trying to tackle the biggest truck out there.
> —Gary Burley

Slide 42

> **Creating Humor with Specific Images**
>
> **General Statement**
> He is hard to tackle.
>
> **Specific Examples with Hyperboles**
> Each time you tackle him, it reduces your I.Q.
> —Pete Wysocki
>
> Every time I tackle him, I hear a dice game going on inside my mouth.
> —Don Burroughs

Review the difference between simile and hyperbole with students using examples in Slides 41 and 42.

Explain to them that their assignment for Activity 5 is to create a color commentary using similes and hyperboles. Emphasize that their color commentary does not have to be humorous. To earn points, the specific examples just need to create an interesting image.

Have the students turn in their color commentaries so that you can review them and select the best to be shared.

An Additional Assignment

Assign students to locate a joke that begins with a generalization and ends with a specific image. The joke can be either short, like the Ron Darian example below, or long, like the Seinfeld cut. Have them underline or boldface the specific image.

Remind students that their selection must be appropriate for sharing.

A Short Example:

> Ants can carry twenty times their own body weight, which is useful information **if you're moving and you need help carrying a potato chip across town.**
> —Ron Darian

A Long Example:

> On my block a lot of people walk their dogs, and I always see them walking along with their little poop bags. This, to me, is the lowest activity in human life. **If aliens are watching this through telescopes, they're going to think the dogs are the leaders of the planet. If you see two life forms, one of them is making a poop, the other one's carrying it for him, who would you assume is in charge?**
> —Jerry Seinfeld

As with the color commentary, you may want to collect this assignment and select the best to be shared.

Image Grammar Teacher Guide
Strategies for the Grammar of Conventions

Researchers have shown that 91.5 percent of all errors in student writing come from only 20 items. Many of these same errors have also been targeted as "status producing," meaning that they cause well-educated individuals in our society to think less of individuals committing these errors.

This section on conventions focuses on 15 errors—a cross between the status producing and the most common errors that students make. The first few strategies introduce a vocabulary of grammatical structures needed to correct errors. The second group of strategies, beginning with the Shalersville University Occupational Inventory, specifically targets these 15 critical errors.

This section is not intended as a comprehensive treatment of all grammatical errors but instead, is designed to target concepts that can help students make the greatest gains in the shortest time, as suggested in the research of Hairston (1982), Connors and Lundsford (1988), and Noguchi (1991).

Slide 1

Slides 2–6

Introduce this section of the PowerPoint with **Slide 1**.

Show **Slides 2–5** and have students create new sentences using the template on page 72 of the Activity Book. Be sure that students keep the articles, prepositions, and conjunctions indicated in blue.

Ask students to share their "real-word" imitations of these patterns. Compare the words they substituted for these nonsense words in the first two sentences: *zan, sorner, tolmer, mooklar, gonkers,* and *pag.* (Slide 6)

Ask if anyone can tell which part of speech all these words represent? Most should be able to recognize that the words in the first group are nouns and the words that match *vogged* and *delted* are verbs. Explain that the ability to match real words with the nonsense words demonstrates the templates in their minds.

Slide 7

Slide 8

Painting the Template Images

Tigoling at the peler zugroo, Roscoe sagored and kaked.
When the zugroo clooted sumly and turked a mook pun at
the wertip, Roscoe berked and veeped, cronking over a putim
and baloking at the nook.

Slide 9

Painting the Template Images

smiled	grinned	beamed	smirked
sneered	mocked	laughed	snickered
gazed	stared	glanced	watched
gawked	analyzed	examined	studied
scrutinized	considered	jogged	trotted
dashed	hustled	scampered	scurried
scrambled	crawled	sauntered	leaped
hopped	vaulted	bounced	bounded
flinched	winced	recoiled	ambushed
pounced	screamed	bellowed	howled
shrieked	bawled	whooped	hooted
screeched	yelped	squealed	

Slide 10

Painting the Template Images

Nouns	Verbs	Adjectives	Adverbs	Participles
zugroo	sagored	peler	sumly	Tigoling
Roscoe	kaked	mook		cronking
zugroo	clooted			baloking
pun	turked			
wertip	berked			
Roscoe	veeped			
putim				
nook				

Remaining words will include these prepositions, articles, and conjunctions: at, the, and, when, the, and, a, at, the, and, over, a, and, at, the.

With the next activity, you might want to have students work in a group, sharing ideas. This can add spontaneous peer teaching as students discuss the image in **Slide 7**. Explain to the class that they will be imitating a nonsense passage about Roscoe, so they will need to examine the image of Roscoe before writing.

Mention that Roscoe is an orangutan. (You may want to write *orangutan* on the board in case your students decide to use that word in their descriptions.) Next ask students to compare the image with the nonsense passage that describes Roscoe. **(Slide 8)**

Tell students that their task is to rewrite the nonsense paragraph, describing Roscoe with real words. Encourage them to use the sample verbs on page 74 in their Activity Books **(Slide 9)** to help them brainstorm Roscoe's activities.

TIP If you just want to enrich your students' image vocabularies as they describe Roscoe, you could allow them to pull some words from their artists' palettes or from any of the sample palettes in Section 1.

After students have completed their descriptions, invite them to share their passages. Then, show **Slide 10** and ask them to fill in the chart on page 75 in their Activitiy Books by writing in the word they used where the nonsense word is located. For example, they should write the word they used for *sagored* in the first slot below the label "Verbs."

Mention that nouns and verbs are used most often because they create the focal point for image descriptions.

Additional Activity Testing with Templates

Slide 11

Template for Identifying Five Structures

(The, A, An) _____ (is, are, was, were) unusual.

The _____ creature was interesting.

The creature(s) _____.

The creature moved _____

_____, the creature surprised us.

Noun

Adjective

Verb

Adverb

Participle

Painting the Template Images

To help students recognize how grammatical structures are slotted in our mental templates, have them test their nouns, verbs, etc., by placing them in the slots in Slide 11.

Explain that students should select from the items in parentheses ( ) to match the word they insert. Also, they should insert an *-ing* word in the participle blank.

These templates can act as an aid to help your students get started. However, they are not intended to be comprehensive guides. Structures such as helping verbs and pronouns, for example, are not included. These and other elements should be introduced later.

Point out that a participle often has a prepositional phrase after it, creating a participle brush stroke such as "diving into the lake," "running across the field," or "thinking about the problem." Also, mention that some words are "shape shifters" and can fit in more than one slot. For example, the word *soaring* can introduce a participial phrase in the sentence, "Soaring through the clouds, the eagle glided toward its nest." But it can also be used as an adjective when used as a single word as in the sentence, "The soaring eagle landed in the tall oak tree."

Earlier in the Activity Book (pages 48–50), students worked with prepositions and subordinate conjunctions to create rhythms of parallel structure. Consider reviewing these as you comment on the chart's remaining words—the articles, prepositions, subordinate conjunctions, and coordinate conjunctions—all of which provide the glue that holds the sentences together.

Slide 12

You're Fired! / You're Hired

Cover Letter Rankings

	Group 1	Group 2	Group 3	Group 4	Group 5
Emma Dyer	___	___	___	___	___
Lulu Kabong	___	___	___	___	___
John Nobel	___	___	___	___	___
Homer Shnoz	___	___	___	___	___
Betty Guesston	___	___	___	___	___
Louis Lamore	___	___	___	___	___

Slide 13

You're Fired! / You're Hired

Number of Grammatical Errors in Each Letter

1 Error	John Nobel
2 Errors	Betty Guesston
3 Errors	Emma Dyer
6 Errors	Homer Shnoz
7 Errors	Louis Lamore
9 Errors	Lulu Kabong

This activity is designed to help students recognize the importance of "correct" grammar. As linguists have demonstrated over the years, the concept of "correctness" is often based on habits of social status rather than a definitive structure of language. However, to successfully interact with educated members of our society, it is important for students to learn our language traditions. What educated members of a society perceive as correct or incorrect grammar can influence their decisions to hire an individual, to grant a promotion, to admit a college applicant, and so forth.

Divide the class into five groups and explain that each group is a personnel team in charge of hiring new employees. To save time reading resumes, these teams have decided to first sort job applicants based on their cover letters. The team will rank each letter from 1 (best) to 6 (worst). Tell the teams that they are searching for competent individuals for a variety of positions, and that each candidate is applying for a different type of job. After the teams have discussed and ranked all six letters, ask them to select a spokesperson to explain why they ranked the letters as they did.

Project **Slide 12** onto a blackboard so you can mark the rankings of each group for comparison.

Mention to the class that usually two factors influence the evaluation of cover letters: (1) the content and (2) the grammatical correctness. Review **Slide 13** and look where groups ranked Lamore, Shnoz, and Kabong. These letters contained the most grammatical errors. Chances are these three were ranked at the bottom of most evaluations. This is not to ignore the content but to show that grammar does play a role.

Ask students if they would agree that the letter writers who ranked in the bottom three categories were probably not as intelligent as the letter writers at the top of the list. This may generate some debate. Although an individual's grammatical patterns have nothing to do with his or her intelligence, people connect the two. Grammatical correctness only reflects the grammatical habits of those around a person, and these habits—unlike intelligence—can be changed.

Slides 14–19

Show students where the errors are in the application letters using **Slides 14–19**.

Finally, have students write an essay, comparing and contrasting their choice of the best letter and the worst. Depending on the writing level of your class, you might want to suggest that students construct a thesis statement and follow it with four paragraphs beginning with "First, Second, In addition," and "Finally." Also, have them use two techniques—brush strokes or parallel structures—in each paragraph.

The Shalersville University Occupational Inventory of Grammatical Knowledge, pages 81-82

Slide 20

The Shalersville University Occupational
Inventory of Grammatical Knowledge

Shalersville University Occupational Inventory
of Grammatical Knowledge Answer Key

1. I	11. I	21. I
2. I	12. I	22. I
3. C	13. I	23. C
4. I	14. C	24. I
5. I	15. I	25. I
6. I	16. I	26. I
7. C	17. I	27. I
8. I	18. I	28. I
9. I	19. C	29. I
10. I	20. I	30. I

Slide 21

The Shalersville University Occupational
Inventory of Grammatical Knowledge

Inventory Rankings

Points Missed	Projected Salary	Occupational Level
0 to -1	$200,000 and above	top executive
-2 to -3	$90,000 to $200,000	upper management
-4 to -5	$60,000 to $90,000	key personnel
-6 to -8	$25,000 to $60,000	semi-skilled
-9 to -10	$10,000 to $25,000	unskilled
-11 or more	$0 to $10,000	unemployable

Use "You're Fired! / You're Hired!" as an introduction to the Shalersville University Occupational Inventory of Grammatical Knowledge on pages 81–82 of the student Activity Book. Review the introduction to the occupational inventory and emphasize to students that this test will predict their future incomes. Tell students that this test will not count for a grade but will help target the grammatical concepts they need to know.

Administer the test and remind students that each answer left blank means the person taking the test admits that he or she does not know the answer. Being honest by leaving a blank counts for a minus one. Each answer that is wrong counts for a minus two. This eliminates credit for guessing since each guess has a fifty-fifty chance of being correct.

To reduce anxiety and possible embarrassment, have students score their own papers using the Answer Key on **Slide 20**. Tell them that they need not share their scores with anyone but you.

Next, show **Slide 21** and have students calculate their projected future salaries.

Many of your students will score in the unemployable category and might moan and groan about their low occupational levels. However, assure them that in the weeks ahead, you are going to raise their incomes by $50,000 (maybe $100,000) if they are willing to learn just fifteen concepts.

Slide 22

The Shalersville University Occupational
Inventory of Grammatical Knowledge

Fifteen of the Most Common Grammatical Errors Identified by Question Number

1 and 11	Subject-Verb Agreement
2 and 12	Double Negatives
3 and 13	Pronoun as Subject and Object
4 and 14	Sentence Fragments
5 and 15	Run-on Sentences/Comma Splices/Fused Sentences
6 and 16	Capitalization of Proper Nouns
7 and 17	Confusion with *sit, set, set*
8 and 18	Confusion with *their* and *they're/your* and *you're/its* and *its*
9 and 19	Comma after an Introductory Element
10 and 20	Lack of Parallel Structure
21 and 26	Possessive Apostrophe Error
22 and 27	Dangling Participle
23 and 28	Commas in a Series
24 and 29	Pronoun and Antecedent
25 and 30	Restrictive and Nonrestrictive Clauses

Slide 23

Strategies for the Grammar of Conventions

I cannot overemphasize the importance of good grammar. Suppose you are being interviewed for a job as an airplane pilot, and your prospective employer asks you if you have any experience, and you answer, "Well, I ain't never actually flied no actual airplanes or nothing, but I got several pilot-style hats and several friends who I like to talk about airplanes with." If you answer this way, the prospective employer will immediately realize that you have ended your sentence with a preposition.

—Dave Barry, "What Is and Ain't Grammatical"

Show the Confidential Score Sheet on Slide 22 and ask students to circle the number of each of the items missed and turn in their score sheets to you. This will provide you with a guide for teaching those items students find most difficult. Hold the class responsible for all of the fifteen items listed but plan to spend more time on those errors that most students missed. For added mini-lesson help, at the end of each collection of concepts, you will find links to a variety of Web sites that contain free additional material to help students. Beware, however, that many of these and other sites are multiple-choice drills, which are useful but not as effective as working with "express line" paragraphs or original student writing. Use the Web sites for definitions and additional examples.

There is one catch to the Shalersville Inventory: the test is pure fiction. There is no Shalersville University or Dr. McCormick, but do not tell the students this until long after they have worked to improve their incomes. At that point, you can honestly say that although there is no such test, there should be. Grammar does count in life. Any individual working in a business where there are opportunities for advancement will tell you that an employee's grammatical conventions influence his or her opportunities for promotion.

There is an amusing Dave Barry comment that you might want to use as an introduction to critical conventions. (Slide 23)

Introduction to the Express Line Checkouts, page 84

To learn all of the grammatical errors that an individual could possibly make would take years. However, we can shortcut this process by focusing on (1) the errors that occur most frequently and (2) the errors that are status producing, meaning that educated individuals easily recognize them. Researchers have shown that 91.5 percent of all errors in student writing come from only 20 items. We are going to examine fifteen of these items using author Jeff Anderson's "Express Line Checkout" approach plus a "Proofreading Warm-up" activity.

Here is how an Express Line Checkout works. Just as your students can quickly check out four or five items in a grocery store express line, they are asked to check out four or five grammatical items when proofreading a paper. The idea is to examine each paper for only a few selected errors. In the activities that follow, students will be introduced to fifteen of the most common and most status-producing errors made by both high school and college students and asked to proofread for a few of these at a time with selected passages.

Once students have gained skill proofreading for all fifteen errors, you should require them to check their own papers for the same fifteen items until they have mastered them. The idea of limiting the study of conventions to a small list of critical concepts was first suggested in 1917 by Roy Van Johnson, who created one of the first lists of the most frequent grammatical errors. Since then, a variety of lists have been developed, ranging from a 1930 list by Paul Witty and Roberta Green of the top ten student errors to a 1988 list by Connors and Lunsford of the twenty most common student errors. In 1982, Hairston added another perspective by classifying the most common errors that influence an individual's social status.

The fifteen grammatical concepts addressed in the Activity Book provide a starting point—a collection of activities that focus on the most common student errors—errors that make up an estimated 85 percent of student grammatical mistakes.

As you introduce these fifteen, you might want to share with students how each error matches two questions on the Shalersville University Occupational Inventory of Grammatical Knowledge. Tell them that each concept they learn will increase their potential income by $15,000 to $30,000.

The Express Line Checkout limits proofreading to just four or five target errors to enable students to have success. If you do an Express Line check regularly with just a few errors each time, students will eventually feel confident about the process. The express checkouts require students to find errors in five Express Line Checkout passages. In addition, the Proofreading Warm-up is a short version of the express checkout, designed to make this process easier for students. By treating the items for both the warm-up and checkout as mini-lesson packages, you can help students see conventions as manageable.

The errors leading up to the checkouts are grouped as follows:

Grammatical Items for Express Line Checkout 1

| 1 and 11 | Subject-Verb Agreement |

Grammatical Items for Express Line Checkout 2

2 and 12	Double Negatives
3 and 13	Pronoun as Subject and Object
4 and 14	Sentence Fragments

Grammatical Items for Express Line Checkout 3

5 and 15	Run-on Sentences / Comma Splices / Fused Sentences
6 and 16	Capitalization of Proper Nouns
7 and 17	Confusion with *Sit, Sat, Set*
8 and 18	Confusion with *Their* and *They're* / *Your* and *You're* / *Its* and *It's*

Grammatical Items for Express Line Checkout 4

9 and 19	Comma After an Introductory Element
10 and 20	Lack of Parallel Structure
21 and 26	Possessive Apostrophe Error

Grammatical Items for Express Line Checkout 5

22 and 27	Dangling Participles
23 and 28	Commas in a Series
24 and 29	Pronoun and Antecedent Agreement
25 and 30	Restrictive and Nonrestrictive Clauses

A key component of this section is the emphasis on the connection between stylistic ideas and traditional conventions. Sentence fragments, for example, are often either unconnected participle brush strokes, unconnected prepositional phrases, or unconnected subordinate conjunction clauses—all discussed in relation to stylistic tools in Sections 1 and 2 of the Activity Book. Dangling participles are often participle brush strokes where students have forgotten to "zoom" in for a close-up on the modified noun, and the lack of parallel structure is a break in the rhythms that students practiced in Section 2, "The Musical Rhythms of Language."

Furthermore, "commas in a series" is introduced in advanced brush strokes and taught again through a variety of parallel structures. The point is that grammatical correctness often creates stylistic grace and power and vice-versa. Use this connection to blend style with correctness as you teach these concepts. Here is a chart to help you emphasize the relationship.

Stylistic Parallels in Eight of the Fifteen Most Common Errors

Problem of Convention	Application of Stylistic Technique
Sentence Fragments	Using participle brush strokes, subordinate conjunction clauses, and prepositional phrases
Capitalization of Proper Nouns	Creating specific nouns and verbs on the lower rungs of the ladder of abstraction
Comma after an Introductory Element	Using participle brush strokes, subordinate conjunction clauses, and prepositional phrases
Lack of Parallel Structure	Designing parallel structures to create musical rhythms
Dangling Participle	Using participle brush strokes correctly—strokes that zoom in for a close-up on the modified noun
Commas in a Series	Creating rhythms with parallel structures and advanced brush strokes
Commas with Restrictive Elements	Creating reverse appositive brush strokes, parallel structures with personal pronouns, and relative pronouns
Restrictive and Nonrestrictive Clauses	Constructing appositive brush strokes adjectives out of order and parallel structures with personal pronouns and relative pronouns

Slide 24

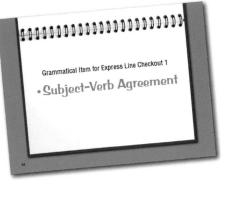

Grammatical Item for Express Line Checkout 1
• Subject-Verb Agreement

Slide 25

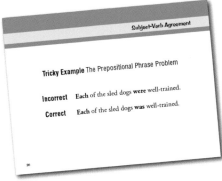

Subject-Verb Agreement

The rule If the subject of a sentence is ONE person, place, thing, or idea, then use a singular verb. If there are MULTIPLE subjects, use a plural verb.

Incorrect His **eyes was** reduced to chinks, and diverging wrinkles appeared round them, extending upon his countenance like the rays in a rudimentary sketch of the rising sun.

Correct His **eyes were** reduced to chinks, and diverging wrinkles appeared round them, extending upon his countenance like the rays in a rudimentary sketch of the rising sun.
—Thomas Hardy

Incorrect He **were** hunted in very much the same fashion as his prototype, the grizzly.
Correct He **was** hunted in very much the same fashion as his prototype, the grizzly.
—Bret Harte

Slide 26

Subject-Verb Agreement

Tricky Example The Prepositional Phrase Problem

Incorrect Each of the sled dogs **were** well-trained.
Correct Each of the sled dogs **was** well-trained.

Slide 27

Subject-Verb Agreement

Tricky Example The Expletive Problem

Incorrect There's no roads of any kind in the valley—nothing but a labyrinth of footpaths twisting and turning among the thickets without end.
Correct There are no roads of any kind in the valley—nothing but a labyrinth of footpaths twisting and turning among the thickets without end.
—Herman Melville

Incorrect There's some things too horrible, too hideous, too repulsive for description—Bukawai's face was one of these.
Correct There are some things too horrible, too hideous, too repulsive for description—Bukawai's face was one of these.
—Edgar Rice Burroughs

Subject-Verb Agreement (Questions 1 and 11)

A few grammatical problems such as subject-verb agreement are more effectively taught as part of the proofreading process. This is why the Express Line Checkout is an essential strategy: it demonstrates the importance of proofreading as part of the writing process.

Introduce the first and perhaps the most complex of the fifteen critical errors—subject-verb agreement (Slide 24). Then review the material in the Activity Book using Slides 25–28.

You might share how Mark Twain portrays Huckleberry Finn as uneducated by having him say this:

> There **was** some **things** which he stretched, but mainly he told the truth.

Ask students why Twain might insert grammatical errors like this into Huckleberry's dialogue. See if they recognize how dialogue in novels and films portrays certain characters as low class. Reinforce the idea that these patterns do not indicate lack of intelligence.

As a double check, have students read the sentence with the prepositional phrase removed and see if they can hear the correct subject-verb combination.

Incorrect   The **group** of performers **were** late to the gig.

Incorrect   The **group were** late to the gig.

Correct   The **group was** late to the gig.

Slide 28

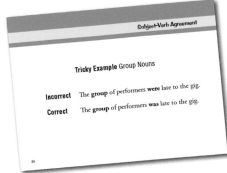

Subject-Verb Agreement

Tricky Example Group Nouns

Incorrect The **group** of performers **were** late to the gig.
Correct The **group** of performers **was** late to the gig.

Slide 29

> Express Line Checkout 1
>
> Uncle Harold was famous for lying. Each of his stories were questionable. There's some stories that I thought were lies for sure, but I enjoyed listening to him.
> He had once been shot right between the eyes. He told me so himself. It was during World War I. As an under-aged boy, he had run away from home, enlisted in the Marine Corps, and been shipped to France. There, a group of the Kaiser's soldiers were tracking him, and eventually one soldier shot him right between the eyes.
> It was a miracle it hadn't killed him, and I said so the evening he told me about it. He explained that Marines on his team was so tough they
> *continued*

Slide 30

> Express Line Checkout 1
>
> didn't need miracles. I was now approaching the age of skepticism, and though it was risky business challenging adults, I was tempted to say, "Swear on the Bible?" I did not dare go this far, but I did get a hint of doubt into my voice by repeating his words as a question.
> "Right between the eyes?"
> "Right between the eyes," he said. "See this scar?"
> He placed a finger on his forehead just above the bridge of his nose.
> "That's all the mark it left," he said.
> "I don't see any scar," I said.
> —Adapted from *Growing Up* by Russell Baker

Slide 31

> Express Line Checkout 1
>
> Uncle Harold was famous for lying.
> He had once been shot right between the eyes. He told me so himself. It was during World War I. An under-aged boy, he had run away from home, enlisted in the Marine Corps, and been shipped to France, where one of the Kaiser's soldiers had shot him. Right between the eyes.
> It was a miracle it hadn't killed him, and I said so the evening he told me about it. He explained that Marines were so tough they didn't need miracles. I was now approaching the age of skepticism, and though it was risky business challenging adults, I was tempted to say, "Swear on the Bible?" I did not dare go this far, but I did get a hint of doubt into my voice by repeating his words as a question.
> "Right between the eyes?"
> "Right between the eyes," he said. "See this scar?"
> He placed a finger on his forehead just above the bridge of his nose. "That's all the mark it left," he said.
> "I don't see any scar," I said.

Answers for Activity 6 are highlighted in red on **Slides 29** and **30**. Also included on the PowerPoint is the original version of the Russell Baker passage. **(Slide 31)** If you read the original to students, explain that Baker uses a fragment (right between the eyes) to give a comic emphasis to this line. Mention that fragments are sometimes used for dramatic purposes, as will be explained in the next Checkout.

Below are some Web sites you might want to investigate for added clarity of definitions and additional examples.

Related Web Sites

http://www.asu.edu/duas/wcenter/subject.html
http://owl.english.purdue.edu/handouts/esl/eslsubverb.html
http://grammar.ccc.commnet.edu/grammar/sv_agr.htm

Slide 32

Grammatical Items for Express Line Checkout 2

• Double Negatives

• Pronoun as Subject and Object

• Sentence Fragments

Use **Slide 32** to emphasize to students that each Express Line Checkout involves only a few items.

Double Negatives (Questions 2 and 12)

To help students avoid the double negative problem, tell them to look for combinations of these words when proofreading: *no, not, none, no one, nothing, nowhere, neither, nobody, never, doesn't, isn't, wasn't, wouldn't, couldn't, shouldn't, won't, can't, don't.* Notice that half of them involve a contraction for "not." When proofreading, look for these contractions. Introduce double negatives with **Slides 33** and **34**.

If you choose to do more with double negatives, try these Web sites: http://www.bbc.co.uk/skillswise/words/grammar/texttypes/negatives and http://www.grammardoctor.com/page3.htm (the history of double negatives).

Pronoun as Subject and Object (Questions 3 and 13)

There are several types of pronoun problems, but to correct subject and object problems, students only need to review pronouns in the two cases explained in the Activity Book.

The "Pronoun as Subject" problem **(Slide 35)** more often occurs with the plural pronoun *they*, as in sentences like "They was coming to the game." Less frequent are errors with singular pronouns, such as "I were coming to the game."

Slide 33

Slide 34

Slide 35

Slide 36

Linking Verbs and Pronouns

Incorrect	It is him.
	This is her.
	It is us who should lead the charge.
Correct	It is he.
	This is she.
	It is we who should lead the charge.

Slide 37

Pronoun as Object

Object of a Preposition
Use *me, her, him, it, us,* and *them* in slots like

The pit bull was near _____.

Slide 38

Pronoun as Subject or Object

Tricky Example The Name-Pronoun Problem

Incorrect	Owen and me were throwing rocks into the Squamscott, the saltwater river.
Correct	Owen and I were throwing rocks into the Squamscott, the saltwater river.
	—John Irving
Incorrect	Leon gave the tickets to Roberto and I.
Correct	Leon gave the tickets to Roberto and me.

Slides 39–41

Proofreading Warm-up

Proofreading Warm-up

Proofreading Warm-up

As we drove nearer, it proved to be, to our excitement, a small herd of six buffalo, hunchbacked, shaggy, wading shoulder high through the snow, packed tightly together, trailing shawls of white steamy breath behind them...
We watched them for perhaps ten minutes until they were out of sight. We were just going to start up the car when suddenly, from the interior of the dark mesh of trees, out strolled an enormous old bull buffalo. On to the snowfield, white as a banqueting-cloth, he sauntered out, his beard swinging to his rolling walk, his horns sharp-curved as bows, his great forehead and massive shoulders a mass of dark ringlets, the breath from his nostrils making two cumulus clouds of steam ahead of him as he moved. Slowly, like a portly, well-made man of substance taking his constitutional, he moved across the white expanse. Here the snow was not so deep, so it only came up to his knees. He moved ponderously across until he was perhaps two hundred yards from the tree line. Then he paused and mused, his breath forming a cloud around his face, entangling itself in the fur of his forehead and shoulders. Then he sauntered after the herd, of which we had no doubt he was king. Slowly, meditatively, like a huge, dark cloud, he moved across the snow and disappeared.

One of the most common errors with subject pronouns occurs when the pronoun renames the subject and follows a linking verb such as *is, are, was, were, am,* and forms of *be*. In this case, the pronoun should be a personal pronoun. There are examples on **Slide 36**.

Explain the use of a pronoun as an object by reviewing the Activity Book explanation on page 89 and using **Slide 37**.

Note that two objective personal pronouns (*you* and *it*) can also function as subjective personal pronouns. You can correctly use these as a subject as in the following:

It was there.

It was brown.

You can also correctly use these two words as objects as in these sentences:

The pit bull was **near it**.

She was surprised **by it**.

Using **Slide 38**, explain to students the rule when the subject is a combination of a name and a pronoun. If students are unsure with sentences where a name and a pronoun are used together, have them review some of the Web sites that follow.

Related Web Sites
http://www.grammarbook.com/grammar/pronoun.asp
http://www.usingenglish.com/quizzes/73.html
http://www.easyenglish.com/lesson.asp?him.txt
http://owl.english.purdue.edu/handouts/grammar/g_pronuse.html

The three inserted errors in the passage by Gerald Durrell are in red type on **Slides 39** and **40**. The original of the piece is on **Slide 41**.

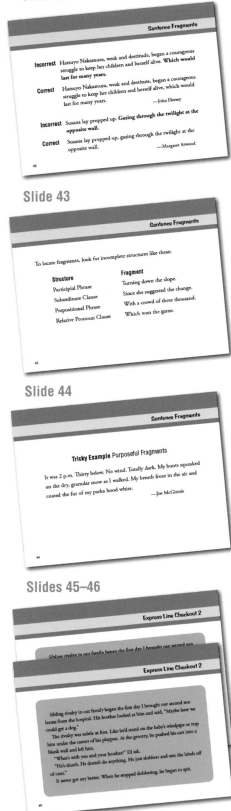

Slide 42

Sentence Fragments

Incorrect Hatsuyo Nakamura, weak and destitute, began a courageous struggle to keep her children and herself alive. **Which would last for many years.**

Correct Hatsuyo Nakamura, weak and destitute, began a courageous struggle to keep her children and herself alive, which would last for many years.
—John Hersey

Incorrect Susana lay propped up. **Gazing through the twilight at the opposite wall.**

Correct Susana lay propped up, gazing through the twilight at the opposite wall.
—Margaret Atwood

Slide 43

Sentence Fragments

To locate fragments, look for incomplete structures like these:

Structure	Fragment
Participial Phrase	Turning down the slope.
Subordinate Clause	Since she suggested the change.
Prepositional Phrase	With a crowd of three thousand.
Relative Pronoun Clause	Which won the game.

Slide 44

Sentence Fragments

Tricky Example Purposeful Fragments

It was 2 p.m. Thirty below. No wind. Totally dark. My boots squeaked on the dry, granular snow as I walked. My breath froze in the air and coated the fur of my parka hood white.
—Joe McGinnis

Slides 45–46

Express Line Checkout 2

Sibling rivalry in our family began the first day I brought our second son

Express Line Checkout 2

Sibling rivalry in our family began the first day I brought our second son home from the hospital. His brother looked at him and said, "Maybe later we could get a dog."
The rivalry was subtle at first. Like he'd stand on the baby's windpipe or trap him under the casters of his playpen. At the grocery, he pushed his cart into a blank wall and left him.
"What's with you and your brother?" I'd ask.
"He's dumb. He doesn't do anything. He just slobbers and eats the labels off of cans."
It never got any better. When he stopped slobbering, he began to spit.

Sentence Fragments (Questions 4 and 14)

While double negatives and pronoun problems are unrelated to style, sentence fragments are mistakes that derive from the unsuccessful use of stylistic elements such as participles and subordinate conjunctions. As you teach these, you can relate them to techniques in Sections 1 and 2 of the Activity Book. Explain how students can often correct fragments by connecting them with a comma to the sentence before or after as in the examples on **Slide 42**.

How can you spot fragments? Fragments usually begin with words that introduce these structures—prepositions, subordinate conjunctions, participles, and relative pronouns. **(Slide 43)** Because they have worked with these structures in Sections 1, 2, and 3 of the Activity Book, students should be able to more easily avoid fragments.

Point out that professional writers sometimes use fragments for effect, as on **Slide 44**. The difference between an error and the correct use of a fragment is that the legitimate fragment has an obvious purpose. Sometimes it creates a rhythmic pattern. Sometimes it provides a tight image that enhances the significance of an idea. However, to avoid confusion, encourage students to avoid all fragments until they can recognize these subtleties.

The inserted errors in the excerpt by Erma Bombeck are highlighted in red on **Slide 45**. The original of the piece is on **Slide 46**.

Related Web Sites

http://www.lessonplanspage.com/
    LASentenceFragmentsInAdsIdea69.htm
http://www.jamestown.k12.nd.us/jhs/writing_tips.htm
http://www.longview.k12.wa.us/mmhs/wyatt/homework/grammar/
    less10.html

Slide 47

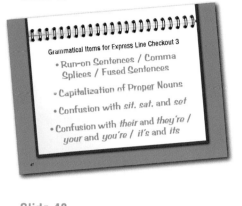

Grammatical Items for Express Line Checkout 3

• Run-on Sentences / Comma Splices / Fused Sentences

• Capitalization of Proper Nouns

• Confusion with *sit*, *sat*, and *set*

• Confusion with *their* and *they're* / *your* and *you're* / *it's* and *its*

Slide 48

Run-on Sentences

A run-on joins two or more sentences with only a coordinating conjunction (*and, but, or, nor, for, so, yet*). The writer leaves out the comma needed with the conjunction to join two sentences.

Incorrect He was emaciated and he was smoking sixty cigarettes a day.

Correct He was emaciated, **and** he was smoking sixty cigarettes a day.
—Truman Capote

Slide 49

Comma Splices

A comma splice joins two sentences with only a comma, as in this incorrect example:

Incorrect A big foaming sea came out of the mist, it made for the ship, roaring wildly and in its rush it looked as mischievous and discomposing as a madman with an axe.

Correct A big foaming sea came out of the mist. It made for the ship, roaring wildly, and in its rush it looked as mischievous and discomposing as a madman with an axe.
—Joseph Conrad

Slide 50

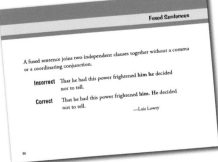

Fused Sentences

A fused sentence joins two independent clauses together without a comma or a coordinating conjunction.

Incorrect That he had this power frightened **him** he decided not to tell.

Correct That he had this power frightened **him**. He decided not to tell.
—Lois Lowry

Slide 47 shows what grammatical items will be covered in this part of the book.

Run-on Sentences / Comma Splices / Fused Sentences (Questions 5 and 15)

Some teachers treat all three of these categories as variations of run-on sentences. However, categorizing these errors as three separate problems can add clarity for students. Use **Slides 48–50** to explain these concepts.

Slide 51

Fused Sentences

Tricky Example *However*

Incorrect In Cleveland there is legislation moving forward to ban people from wearing pants that fit too low, however, there is a lot of opposition from the plumbers' union.

Correct In Cleveland there is legislation moving forward to ban people from wearing pants that fit too low; however, there is a lot of opposition from the plumbers' union.
—Conan O'Brien

One of the most common errors with comma splices is the use of *however* as a coordinating conjunction. Explain that the word *however* does not join sentences. It must have a semicolon with it when located between sentences. *However* is an interrupter like *furthermore*. Show the example on Slide 51.

Related Web Sites

http://leo.stcloudstate.edu/punct/avcsfsro.html

http://www.longview.k12.wa.us/mmhs/wyatt/homework/grammar/
less10.html

http://writing2.richmond.edu/writing/wweb/runon.html

http://www.delmar.edu/engl/wrtctr/obstacle.ppt#2

The inserted errors in the passage by Jean Shepherd are highlighted in red on Slide 52. Slide 53 shows the original version of the piece.

You might want to point out the examples of fragments used for comic effect in this passage. ("Pow." and "Just like that.") The use of fragments was described in earlier examples with Baker's piece on Uncle Harold and the section on fragments.

Slide 52

Proofreading Warm-up

BLAM!
The kitchen door flew open, it had been left ajar just a crack to let the air come in to cool the ham. I rushed to the kitchen, however, just in time to see the blue-ticked Bumpus hounds roar through the screen door in a great, rolling mob the leader of the pack—the one that almost got the old man every day—leaped high onto the table and grabbed the butt end of the ham in his enormous slavering jaws. The rest of the hounds—squealing, yapping, panting, rolling over one another in a frenzy of madness—pounded out the kitchen door after Big Red, trailing brown sugar and pineapple slices behind him. They were in and out in less than five seconds. The screen door hung on one hinge, its screen ripped and torn and dripping with gravy and they went out just like that.
—Adapted from *A Christmas Story* by Jean Shepherd

Slide 53

Proofreading Warm-up

BLAM!
The kitchen door flew open. It had been left ajar just a crack to let the air come in to cool the ham. I rushed to the kitchen just in time to see the blue-ticked Bumpus hounds roar through the screen door in a great, rolling mob. The leader of the pack—the one that almost got the old man every day—leaped high onto the table and grabbed the butt end of the ham in his enormous slavering jaws. The rest of the hounds—squealing, yapping, panting, rolling over one another in a frenzy of madness—pounded out the kitchen door after Big Red, trailing brown sugar and pineapple slices behind him. They were in and out in less than five seconds. The screen door hung on one hinge, its screen ripped and torn and dripping with gravy. Out they went. Pow. Just like that.

Creating Proper Nouns, pages 96-98

Slide 54

Common Noun	Proper Noun
musical group	
television program	
famous artist	
language	
city	
historical event	
sports figure	
movie title	
favorite team	
friend's name	
book title	

Proper Nouns

54

Slide 55

Proper Nouns

Tricky Example Proper Adjectives

Adjectives Created from Proper Nouns:
American, German, Mexican (ending in –an or –ian)

Exceptions:
French, Chinese

55

Capitalization of Proper Nouns (Questions 6 and 16)

Review the ladder of abstraction activity in "Section 3: Specific Details: The Close-up Power of the Zoom Lens." The earlier work with specific nouns should have provided a good foundation for introducing proper and common nouns. See how well students are able to create proper nouns from the list of common nouns on Slide 54.

Have students share their answers to the activity.

When Activity 10 is complete, teach a mini-lesson on how proper adjectives are derived from proper nouns. (Slide 55)

Related Web Sites

http://www.yorku.ca/gcareers/grammar/capital_letters.htm
http://englishplus.com/grammar/00000045.htm
http://www.rhlschool.com/eng3n1.htm

Slide 56

> **Commonly Confused Words**
>
> *Sit* means to rest.
>   Sit down and relax.
>
> *Sat* is something that already has happened.
>   She sat here yesterday.
>
> *Set* can be replaced with the word *put*.
>   Set the book on the table.
>
> 56

Slide 57

> **Commonly Confused Words**
>
> **Match the Word with the Blank**
>   *sit   set   sat*
>
> Shanna _____ her glass on the edge of the table.
>
> Last week, Deron _____ on the soft recliner.
>
> I watched the cat _____ by the fire.
>
> 57

Slide 58

> **Commonly Confused Words**
>
> **Answers**
>
> Shanna set her glass on the edge of the table.
>
> Last week, Deron sat on the soft recliner.
>
> I watched the cat sit by the fire.
>
> 58

Slide 59

> **Commonly Confused Words**
>
> **Confusion with *their* and *they're***
>
> To check if you have used the right word, just substitute the full verb for the apostrophe *s* or the apostrophe *re* and see if the sentence works.
>
> Incorrect   They're house was cold.
>
> Incorrect   They are house was cold.
>
> Correct   Their house was cold.
>
> 59

Confusion with *Sit, Sat, Set* (Questions 7 and 17)

Review this with Slide 56 and emphasize the idea of testing for *set* by replacing it with *put*.

The following is a brief exercise, not an activity. Show Slide 57 and have students give an answer with an explanation based on the information in the previous slide. Move back and forth between Slide 56 and Slide 57 to help students. Answers for the exercise are on Slide 58.

Related Web Sites

http://www.lessontutor.com/eessit.html
http://www.uhv.edu/ac/student/writing/grammartip111504.html
http://www.english-zone.com/verbs/set.html

Confusion with *their* and *they're* / *your* and *you're* / *its* and *it's* (Questions 8 and 18)

Review these often confused words with students. (Slide 59)

Note: You may also want to introduce *there*, although it is not as often confused as *their* and *they're*. *There* indicates a place or situation as in these examples:

My friend is over **there**.

There is a gorilla on the roof.

Related Web Sites

http://www.better-english.com/easier/theyre.htm
http://www.gcse.com/english/there.htm
http://www.usingenglish.com/handouts/75.html

Slide 60

> Among my experiments was this, in an hour I taught a cat and a dog to be friends. I sat them in a cage. In another hour I taught them to be friends with a rabbit. In the course of two days I was able to add a fox, a goose, a squirrel, some doves, and finally a monkey. They lived together in peace, even affectionately.
>
> Next, in another cage I confined an Irish Catholic from Tipperary, and as soon as he seemed tame, I added a scotch Presbyterian from Aberdeen. Next, I added a Turk from Constantinople; a Greek Christian from Crete; an Armenian; a Methodist from the wilds of arkansas; a Buddhist from China;
>
> *continued*

Slide 61

> a Brahman from Benares, and finally, a Salvation Army Colonel from Wapping. Then I stayed away two whole days, when I came back to note results, the cage of animals was all right, but in the other their was but a chaos of gory odds and ends of turbans and fezzes and plaids and bones and flesh—not a specimen left alive. These reasoning animals had disagreed on a theological detail and carried the matter to a higher court.
>
> —Adapted from *Letters from the Earth* by Mark Twain

Slide 62

> Among my experiments was this. In an hour I taught a cat and a dog to be friends. I put them in a cage. In another hour I taught them to be friends with a rabbit. In the course of two days I was able to add a fox, a goose, a squirrel, some doves, and finally a monkey. They lived together in peace—even affectionately.
>
> Next, in another cage I confined an Irish Catholic from Tipperary, and as soon as he seemed tame, I added a Scotch Presbyterian from Aberdeen. Next, I added a Turk from Constantinople; a Greek Christian from Crete; an Armenian; a Methodist from the wilds of Arkansas; a Buddhist from China; a Brahman from Benares, and finally, a Salvation Army Colonel from Wapping.
>
> *continued*

Slide 63

> Then I stayed away two whole days. When I came back to note results, the cage of animals was all right, but in the other there was but a chaos of gory odds and ends of turbans and fezzes and plaids and bones and flesh—not a specimen left alive. These reasoning animals had disagreed on a theological detail and carried the matter to a higher court.

The inserted errors in this short passage by Mark Twain are highlighted in red on **Slides 60** and **61**. The original passage can be seen on **Slides 62** and **63**.

Grammatical Items for Express Line Checkout 4, pages 100-104

Slide 64

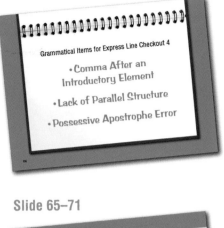

Grammatical Items for Express Line Checkout 4

- Comma After an Introductory Element
- Lack of Parallel Structure
- Possessive Apostrophe Error

Introduce this Checkout with Slide 64.

Comma After an Introductory Element (Questions 9 and 19)

Illustrate the comma rules with examples from Slides 65 to 71.

Students should begin to see how participles, prepositions, and subordinate conjunctions serve two functions: correctness and style.

Slide 65-71

Introductory Element

Single Introductory Word

Introductory Element

Long Introductory Prepositional Phrase

Introductory Element

Short Introductory Prepositional Phrase

Introductory Element

Introductory Participle Brush Stroke

Running along the ramparts, bent double, the Abbot

Introductory Element

Introductory Clause with a Subordinate Conjunction

Introductory Element

Tricky Example *Gerund Phrase*

Introductory Element

Participle Brush Stroke Intact	Running along the ramparts, bent double, the Abbot cried out, "Stretcher bearers! Over here!" —Brian Jacques
Participle Brush Stroke Eliminated	Bent double, the Abbot cried out, "Stretcher bearers! Over here!"

ACTIVITY 12 Proofreading Warm-up, page 102

Slide 72

Slide 73

Introduced errors in the passage by Jay Leno are circled in red on **Slide 72**. The original of the passage is on **Slide 73**.

Related Web Sites

http://www.grammartips.homestead.com/adverbs1.html
http://grammar.ccc.commnet.edu/grammar/commas_intro.htm

Slides 74–75

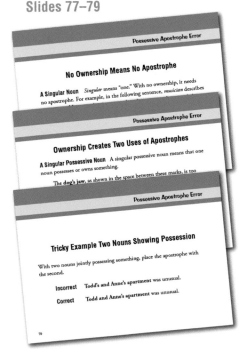

Lack of Parallel Structure

Broken Rhythm   The slow, quiet winter was spent telling stories,

Lack of Parallel Structure

Broken Rhythm   She cocked her head and narrowed her eyes, and
she was twisting her lips in a fashion that said,
"Irv, Calm down."

Melodic Rhythm   She cocked her head and narrowed her eyes
and twisted her lips in a fashion that said,
"Irv, Calm down."
—Tom Wolff

Slide 76

Possessive Apostrophe Error

Magee-Womens Hospital
Nail's by Deca
Your all fool's.
Lab puppy's for sale

Slides 77–79

Possessive Apostrophe Error

No Ownership Means No Apostrophe

A Singular Noun   *Singular* means "one." With no ownership, it needs
no apostrophe. For example, in the following sentence, *musician* describes

Possessive Apostrophe Error

Ownership Creates Two Uses of Apostrophes

A Singular Possessive Noun   A singular possessive noun means that one
noun possesses or owns something.

The dog's jaw, as shown in the space between these marks, is too

Possessive Apostrophe Error

Tricky Example Two Nouns Showing Possession

With two nouns jointly possessing something, place the apostrophe with
the second.

Incorrect   Todd's and Anne's apartment was unusual.

Correct   Todd and Anne's apartment was unusual.

Lack of Parallel Structure (Questions 10 and 20)

The most common error with parallel structure is a broken rhythm. This is created when a pattern is established and then broken. There are two examples of this problem on Slides 74 and 75.

This is a difficult problem to solve because it derives from the student's lyrical sense—a quality that comes from extensive reading. In some ways learning the music of parallel structures is analogous to learning melodies well enough to hum them.

Related Web Sites

http://wwwnew.towson.edu/ows/modulePARALLEL.htm
http://www.wilbers.com/part40.htm
http://owl.english.purdue.edu/handouts/grammar/g_parallel.html
http://www.english.vt.edu/~IDLE/gym2/workout18/
        w18.stretch1.html

Possessive Apostrophe Error (Questions 21 and 26)

Slide 76 provides an amusing way to introduce the problems of the apostrophe. These examples were spotted by a journalist and a freelance writer on their way to work.

Review the explanations for apostrophe errors on Slides 77–79.

Related Web Sites

http://www.uhv.edu/ac/grammar/apostrophes.html
http://www.english.vt.edu/~owl/wcip/gramhndbk.htm#apos
http://owl.english.purdue.edu/handouts/grammar/g_apostEX1.html

Slide 80

> **Express Line Checkout 4**
>
> **The Struggle of Women Artists**
>
> When art was at its peak in Italy during the fifteenth and sixteenth century only men were recognized as artists. Women were viewed as lacking in intelligence, lacking in character and they didn't have enough fortitude. Art academies refused to admit them. Their status in Italian society was comparable to that of a slave.
>
> The popular perception at that time was that women were only good for cleaning, child bearing, and to cook. Any woman who attempted to create art was considered scandalous. Womens rights were nonexistent. Consequently, only a few women in that time period were able to develop as artists, and most of these learned from their fathers who were painters. When a woman did emerge as a master artist very few patrons would buy her art. The women artist's had no choice but to concentrate on one type of painting—the portrait, considered at the time as an inferior artistic expression, rarely done by serious artists. *continued*

The errors in the short article entitled "The Struggle of Women Artists" are highlighted in red on Slides 80 and 81. The original version of the article is on Slides 82 and 83.

Slide 81

> **Express Line Checkout 4**
>
> Female artists like Frida Kahlo, Kathe Kollwitz, and Georgia O'Keeffe are now regarded as some of history's very best. Yet, some injustices continue today. For example, art history books until only recently have excluded most woman artists. Similarly museum collections for centuries only exhibited male artists.
>
> Fortunately, women are mobilizing to rectify these inequities. In 1985 a group of American women artists founded the Guerilla Girls. Members assumed the names of dead women artists and spread their quest for fairness through billboards, books, plays, workshops, and demonstrations. To attract publicity and focus media attention on issues, the Guerilla Girls wore gorilla masks at demonstrations. Recently the group has grown to over 100 members and has expanded their concerns beyond art to include issues involving sexism, involving racism, and to help social injustice.

Slide 82

> **Express Line Checkout 4**
>
> **The Struggle of Women Artists** *Errors Corrected*
>
> When art was at its peak in Italy during the fifteenth and sixteenth century, only men were recognized as artists. Women were viewed as lacking in intelligence, lacking in character, and lacking in fortitude. Art academies refused to admit them. Their status in Italian society was comparable to that of a slave.
>
> The popular perception at that time was that women were only good for cleaning, child bearing, and cooking. Any woman who attempted to create art was considered scandalous. Women's rights were nonexistent. Consequently, only a few women in that time period were able to develop as artists, and most of these learned from their fathers who were painters. When a woman did emerge as a master artist, very few patrons would buy her art. The women artists had no choice but to concentrate on one type of painting—the portrait, considered at the time as an inferior artistic expression, rarely done by serious artists. *continued*

Slide 83

> **Express Line Checkout 4**
>
> Female artists like Frida Kahlo, Kathe Kollwitz, and Georgia O'Keeffe are now regarded as some of history's very best. Yet, some injustices continue today. For example, art history books until only recently have excluded most woman artists. Similarly, museum collections for centuries only exhibited male artists.
>
> Fortunately, women are mobilizing to rectify these inequities. In 1985, a group of American women artists founded the Guerilla Girls. Members assumed the names of dead women artists and spread their quest for fairness through billboards, books, plays, workshops, and demonstrations. To attract publicity and focus media attention on issues, the Guerilla Girls wore gorilla masks at demonstrations. Recently, the group has grown to over 100 members and has expanded their concerns beyond art to include issues involving sexism, involving racism, and social injustice.

Grammatical Items for
Express Line Checkout 5, pages 106-111

Slide 84

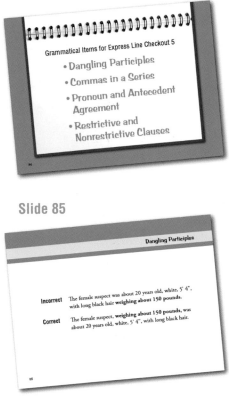

Slide 85

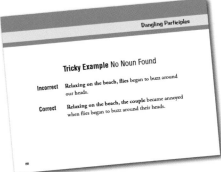

Slide 86

Introduce the focus of this Checkout with Slide 84.

Dangling Participles (Questions 22 and 27)

Review the procedure for painting participle brush strokes. Explain to students that if a participle brush stroke is not located close to the noun being painted, the meaning of the sentence can be jumbled, sometimes with comic effect. Show Slides 85–86.

Tell students: "To avoid a dangling participle, think of yourself as a word painter and paint your brush stroke in the sentence, close to the noun image you want to embellish."

Related Web Sites

http://lbarker.orcon.net.nz/hangingparticiple.html

http://www.usu.edu/markdamen/WritingGuide/10dangpt.htm

http://home.bluemarble.net/~langmin/miniatures/dangling.htm

Grammatical Items for Express Line Checkout 5, pages 106–111 (cont.)

Slides 87–91

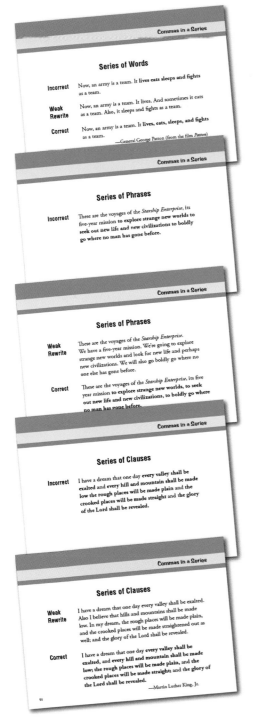

Commas in a Series (Questions 23 and 28)

Review a few of the concepts presented in the advanced brush strokes in Section 1 and in the parallel structures in Section 2. Both illustrate the use of commas in a series. Included with each of the comma examples is a "weak rewrite" to demonstrate what happens when parallel structures break down. Show Slides 87–91.

Consider introducing infinitives and the *asyndeton* using the *Star Trek* introduction on page 107 of the Activity Book as an example. *Asyndeton* is a Greek term for sentence structures in which the word *and* is omitted after the last comma in a parallel series. For example, the *Star Trek* scriptwriter does this by not placing the word *and* after the comma following the word *civilizations*. To show this example on the PowerPoint, refer back to Slide 88.

Related Web Sites

http://www.americanrhetoric.com/figures/parallelism.htm (Good site for examples of parallel structures and sample speeches)
http://depts.dyc.edu/learningcenter/owl/conjunctions.htm
http://grammar.uoregon.edu/conjunctions/subordinating.html

Slide 92

Slide 93

Slide 94

Slide 95

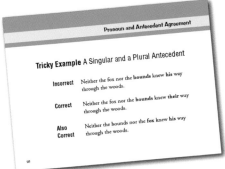

Students should have no difficulty locating three examples, but they probably will not recognize the *-ed* participle *wrapped*. This would be a good opportunity to introduce or reintroduce *-ed* versions of participles. Also, you may want to point out Wiesel's use of an asyndeton. (See Commas in a Series, page 79 of this Teacher Guide.) The word *and* is omitted after *compassion* and *dreams*, where it would normally be included. Authors often omit *and* with parallel structures to enhance the dramatic cadence of the rhythm, as in this sentence by Harlan Ellison:

> "Don't come back till you have him!" the Ticktockman said, **very quietly, very sincerely, extremely dangerously.**

The answers for Activity 14 are in red on Slides 92–93.

Note once again the use of a fragment in Wiesel's comment, "A strange and unnatural state in which the lines blur between light and darkness, dusk and dawn, crime and punishment, cruelty and compassion, good and evil."

Agreement Between Pronoun and Antecedent (Questions 24 and 29)

This problem brings us full circle to the subject-verb, plural-singular relationship discussed earlier. The concept of singular and plural that arises with pronouns and their antecedents is similar to the subject-verb situation.

In both cases, students need to review enough examples so that they can easily recognize plural and singular forms. It would be beneficial with this problem to use additional resources from Internet sites. Explain the concept using Slides 94 and 95.

Related Web Sites
http://englishplus.com/grammar/00000070.htm
http://www.dailygrammar.com/346to350.shtml
http://wwwnew.towson.edu/ows/pro_antagree.htm

Slide 96

Restrictive and Nonrestrictive Clauses (Questions 25 and 30)

Review restrictive and nonrestrictive clauses with Slides 96–98.

Related Web Sites

http://writing-program.uchicago.edu/resources/complex-sentences.htm#restrictive

http://www.getitwriteonline.com/archive/103103.htm

http://www.asu.edu/english/englished/docs/Restrictive_Clauses_pp_27-28.pdf

Slide 97

Slide 98

ACTIVITY 15 Express Line Checkout 5, page 112

Slide 99

> **Express Line Checkout 5**
>
> **Global Warming: A Threat Greater than Terrorism?**
> Not all scientists agree on the cause of global warming, but few deny its existence. Examining the wide range of data, our planet appears to be warming at an alarming rate. The Arctic ice thickness, for example, has shrunk from ten feet to six in less than 30 years. The Artic surface ice has shrunk by 250 million acres—an area as large as California Texas and Maryland combined.
> Projections of the warming trend on our planet vary. Scientists believe by 2100 the earth's temperature could range anywhere from 2.5 to 10 degrees warmer. Each of these projections has their discouraging outcomes. However, all indicate that even the lowest projected temperature increase would create a chain reaction of warming ocean waters that would in turn lead to more frequent hurricanes.
> *continued*

On **Slides 99** and **100**, highlighted in red, are the errors in the short article on global warming. The corrected version of the article is on **Slides 101** and **102**.

Slide 100

> **Express Line Checkout 5**
>
> Meteorologists note that the deadliest hurricanes which are category 4 and 5 have occurred in the last fifteen years. In that same time span, hurricanes have also increased in frequency. From 1970 until 1985, across the entire planet hurricanes averaged 10 per year. From 1990 until 2000 the average rate of hurricanes almost doubled, increasing to 18 per year.
> Professor Peter Webster, MIT graduate and expert on atmospheric and ocean dynamics, believes the increased frequency of hurricanes was due to an ocean water rise in temperature of only .5 degrees Fahrenheit. This slight rise in temperature has already caused the costly destruction of buildings the irreparable damage to coral reefs a dramatic increase in heat-triggered diseases and a significant number of coastal deaths. Consequently, futurists have suggested that global warming will eventually be recognized as a greater threat than terrorism.
> —Written with included errors by Harry Noden

Slide 101

> **Express Line Checkout 5**
>
> **Global Warming: A Threat Greater than Terrorism?** Errors Corrected
> Not all scientists agree on the cause of global warming, but few deny its existence. Examining the wide range of data, most authorities recognize that our planet appears to be warming at an alarming rate. The Arctic ice thickness, for example, has shrunk from ten feet to six in less than 30 years. The Arctic surface ice has shrunk by 250 million acres—an area as large as California, Texas, and Maryland combined.
> Projections of the warming trend on our planet vary. Scientists believe by 2100 the earth's temperature could range anywhere from 2.5 to 10 degrees warmer. Each of these projections has its discouraging outcomes. However, all indicate that even the lowest projected temperature increase would create a chain reaction of warming ocean waters that would in turn lead to more frequent hurricanes.
> *continued*

Slide 102

> **Express Line Checkout 5**
>
> Meteorologists note that the deadliest hurricanes, which are category 4 and 5, have occurred in the last fifteen years. In that same time span, hurricanes have also increased in frequency. From 1970 until 1985, across the entire planet hurricanes averaged 10 per year. From 1990 until 2000 the average rate of hurricanes almost doubled, increasing to 18 per year.
> Professor Peter Webster, MIT graduate and expert on atmospheric and ocean dynamics, believes the increased frequency of hurricanes was due to a rise in the ocean's temperature of only .5 degrees Fahrenheit. This slight rise in temperature has already caused the costly destruction of buildings, the irreparable damage to coral reefs, a dramatic increase in heat-triggered diseases, and a significant number of coastal deaths. Consequently, futurists have suggested that global warming will eventually be recognized as a greater threat than terrorism.

Showtime Performance, pages 113-117

Slide 103

Slide 104

Showtime Performance Rubric

Writing First Draft and Revision

Identify in the margin of your paper **at least one** of each of the following stylistic structures and draw a line from your label to the example.

_____ 1. A Participle Brush Stroke
_____ 2. Adjectives Out-of-Order
_____ 3. An Absolute Brush Stroke
_____ 4. An Appositive Brush Stroke
_____ 5. Use of Specific Nouns and Verbs
_____ 6. Parallel Structure (possibly with prepositional phrases)
_____ 7. Action Verbs (no more than three linking verbs)

Slide 105

Showtime Performance Rubric

Proofreading Common Errors

Check your paper for each of the following structures. (You will receive 10 points for each type of error **not** found in your paper.)

_____ 8. Dangling Participles
_____ 9. Sentence Fragments
_____ 10. Run-ons
_____ 11. Incorrect Use of Comma after an Introductory Element
_____ 12. Breaking the Rhythm of Parallel Structure
_____ 13. Incorrect Use of Commas in a Series
_____ 14. Incorrect Use of Comma with a Restrictive Element

Show **Slide 103** and encourage students to share ideas about a description of the image.

Guidelines for the Showtime Performance Activity
With this activity, follow several steps:

1. Have students describe the image of the band as vividly as possible, imagining what might have happened before and after the photo was taken.

2. After they have written their rough drafts, have them do a first revision, adding stylistic elements listed in the rubric under the subtitle "Writing: First Draft and Revision."

3. Next, have students edit their descriptions by examining a second group of items in the rubric entitled "Proofreading: Common Errors."

Before copying their final versions into their Activity Books, encourage students to review their work and make all additions and revisions on scratch paper.

Use the rubric on **Slides 104–105** to evaluate your students' themes. Remind them to mark each stylistic technique they use in the margin and draw an arrow to the example. Have them also check for grammatical errors, using the second section of the rubric as a guide. This activity is the culmination of all the earlier activities and establishes a pattern for having students integrate concepts of style with concepts of conventions. For some students this will be a difficult activity and may require some additional review.

Have students write at least one additional description from another image. Additional images can be found at http://www.uakron.edu/noden. Be sure students use the same rubric so that the style-convention parallels are reinforced.

Fumblerules, page 118

Slide 106

Fumblerules

1. Verbs has to agree in number with their subjects.
2. Don't use no double negatives.
3. Just between you and I, the case of pronouns is important.
4. About sentence fragments. You should avoid them.
5. Don't use run-on sentences you must punctuate them.
6. Capitalize proper nouns like the mississippi river.
7. Set down and read this list.

continued

106

Slide 107

Fumblerules

8. Their the best burgers in town.
9. When writing an author should use commas for introductory elements.
10. Its important to use apostrophes right in everybodys writing.
11. Being bad grammar, a writer should not use dangling participles.
12. In letters essays and reports use commas to separate items in a series.
13. Make sure each pronoun agrees with their antecedent.
14. Commas shouldn't be used with items, that are restrictive.

107

Fumblerules add a humorous yet educational conclusion to the examination of common grammatical errors. Although George L. Trigg first published a list of Fumblerules, William Safire popularized the term in both his columns and in a book by the same title. Both Trigg and Safire collected samples from a variety of sources. The examples on page 118 are taken from a variety of Web sites. The errors in the examples are highlighted in red on **Slides 106** and **107**.

For more on fumblerules: http://www.yaelf.com/aueFAQ/miffmblrlsdntsndbl.shtml

The Final Frontier

 If you wish, you can give students a final exam on this section by (1) repeating the Shalersville University Occupational Inventory of Grammatical Knowledge and (2) assigning a second Showtime Performance Activity with an image from http://www.uakron.edu/noden. This *Image Grammar* Web site is a companion to the book for teachers entitled *Image Grammar*. Here you will find 101 pages of handout materials, 74 *Image Grammar* lesson strategies, 54 photos, and 92 links to Web sites rich in images.

The *Image Grammar Activity Book*, designed for students, is an extension of the concepts in the book *Image Grammar*, designed for teachers.